TEST YOUR SKILLS IN
PYTHON
LANGUAGE

SHIVANI GOEL

BPB PUBLICATIONS

Distributors:

BPB PUBLICATIONS
20, Ansari Road, Darya Ganj
New Delhi-110002
Ph: 23254990/23254991

DECCAN AGENCIES
4-3-329, Bank Street,
Hyderabad-500195
Ph: 24756967/24756400

COMPUTER BOOK CENTRE
12, Shrungar Shopping Centre,
M.G.Road, BENGALURU–
560001 Ph: 25587923/25584641

BPB BOOK CENTRE
376 Old Lajpat Rai Market,
Delhi-110006
Ph: 23861747

MICRO MEDIA
Shop No. 5, Mahendra Chambers, 150
DN Rd. Next to Capital Cinema, V.T.
(C.S.T.) Station, MUMBAI-400 001 Ph:
22078296/22078297

Published by Manish Jain for BPB Publications, 20, Ansari Road, Darya Ganj, New Delh
110002 and Printed him at Repro India Pvt. Ltd, Mumbai

ARE YOU A PYTHONIST?
TEST YOUR SKILLS IN PYTHON

The Zen of Python:

"Beautiful is better than ugly.
Explicit is better than implicit.
Simple is better than complex.
Complex is better than complicated.
Flat is better than nested.
Sparse is better than dense.
Readability counts.
Special cases aren't special enough to break the rules.
Although practicality beats purity.
Errors should never pass silently.
Unless explicitly silenced. "

---- Tim Peters

About the author

Dr Shivani Goel is an educator and researcher since last 17 years. She has done graduation, post-graduation and doctorate in Computer Science and Engineering from Thapar University, Patiala, Punjab, India. Presently she is Professor at Bennett University, Greater Noida, U.P., India. Her research areas are artificial intelligence, software engineering, algorithms, data structures and programming. She has guided many theses at post graduate and doctorate level. She has more than 60 research publications in International/National Conferences and reputed Journals. Counselling students and motivating them for better learning is her passion. She is also part of projects for designing MOOCs for better education in engineering.

Preface

In this changing world, new programming languages are coming up and curriculum is revised to help students learn the latest trends. I was to teach Python in July 2016 to first year students for the first time. I was on a new journey to learning Python. I found it really interesting. I came up with an idea to write a book for learning in a simple way. I always find a book on question answers as a good approach to learning. So I collected more than 400 questions on all the topics learned. Many questions on one topic in one chapter help the reader in getting a holistic view on a particular topic. This collection of questions is from my own experience of learning through reading books, visiting online websites on Python and teaching with my colleagues at Bennett University.

To get complete benefits, the reader should read first **Getting Started**. The novice users should read all the chapters in the given sequence because all the topics required in a chapter are discussed in all proceeding chapters. However, readers who know Python can jump to any chapter for testing their skills in that topic. The detailed explanation provided along with answers help the reader in understanding the concepts. Model test papers add theory part and programs as well.

My best wishes to all my readers for a successful journey to programming in Python.

Acknowledgements

I would like to thank Almighty for giving me desire and strength to write this book. I am grateful to all my mentors for guiding me through all phases of life.

I dedicate this book to all my mentors and students.

I am thankful to all members of my family for their unconditional love, encouragement and kind support. My special thanks to my loving daughters Gariyasi, Prakriti and caring husband Deepak.

I am thankful to father Sh. Ramesh Chand Goel and brother Vishal Goel for giving me valuable feedback for improving the contents and layout of this book.

I would also like to thank all my colleagues at Bennett University for sharing their learning.

I would also like to thank BPB publications for publishing this work and making my dream come true.

Getting Started

Before beginning journey to programming in Python, we need to note important steps:

1. Download python from www.python.org and install as par the instructions given on the website for your operating system. Say for windows it is stored in folder C:\python35.

    Note: We have executed all programs/commands in version 3.5.2 for windows. Some of the conventions may not work in different versions.

2. Set **Python path variable** in window's class path variable by adding using **My Computer>Properties>Advanced System Settings>Environment Variables> Path Variable> Edit> ;C:\Python35** (in the end of current value). This can also be done while downloading Python.

3. This enables you to run python interpreter by calling **python.exe** on command line or **Start Python IDLE** (in windows) and execute programs saved from any folder in your computer.

4. To run any command in Python, type it in Python shell window:

    >>> print ("Welcome to Python")

    You will see the following Python shell window

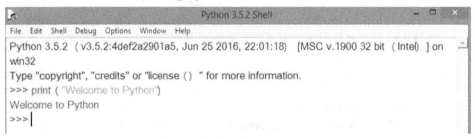

Figure 1 - *Python 3.5.2 Shell*

5. To exit from the python interpreter, press **ctrl+D** or **File→Exit**.

6. The menus in Python Shell window helps in performing various tasks. File handling functions like creating a new file, opening an existing one and saving can be done using File menu. In order to write a Python program, open Python editor window using the following in Python shell: **File→New**

The program is to be written in editor window and saved with a filename with extension .py say **for.py** :

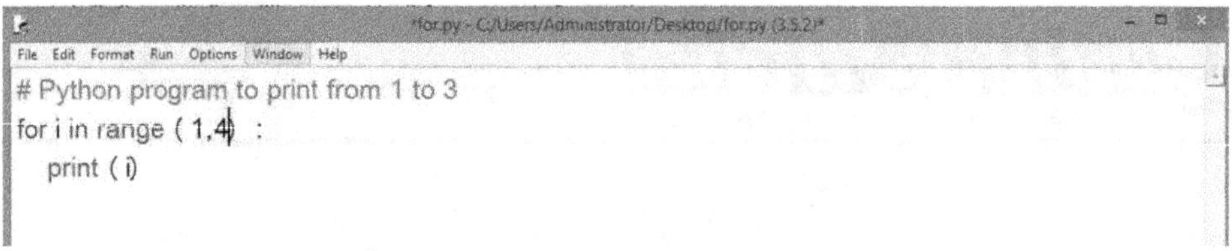

Figure 2. *Python 3.5.2 Editor Window*

7. To execute the program, choose **File→Run (Module)** or **press F5** in editor window. If more programs are written in a single file, it executes all. The output will be shown in Python shell window:

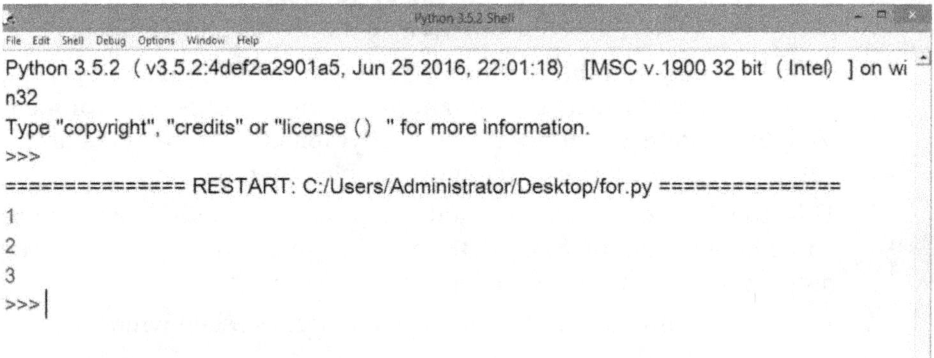

Figure 3. *Program output in Python 3.5.2 Shell*

8. The IDLE of Python can be configured using **Options→Configure IDLE**. The user can set the font size, color indentation etc. according to his/her choice.
9. Python is a case sensitive language i.e. lowercase and uppercase letters are different. All the statements in the body of a statement (decision control, loop, function or class) should be indented.
10. For any help on any topic, **press F1** or use **Help Python Docs** in Python shell or refer to websites given in bibliography.

Contents

S.No.	Topic	Page No.
Chapter 1	Input–Output	1
Chapter 2	Operators and Expressions	7
Chapter 3	Decision Control statements	13
Chapter 4	Loops	21
Chapter 5	Functions	31
Chapter 6	Lists	41
Chapter 7	Strings	48
Chapter 8	Sets and Dictionaries	56
Chapter 9	Tuples	62
Chapter 10	Classes	65
Chapter 11	Files	75
Chapter 12	Graphics	85
Chapter 13	In-built functions	90
Chapter 14	Miscellaneous	96
Appendix A: Python keywords and their use		101
Appendix B: Operators in Python and their precedence		108
Appendix C: Libraries in Python and common functions		110
Bibliography		111
Model Test Paper 1 (Solved)		112
Model Test Paper 2 (Solved)		118
Model Test Paper 3 (Solved)		126
Model Test Paper 4 (Solved)		132
Model Test Paper 5 (Unsolved)		138

Chapter 1

Input-Output

> *In this chapter, you need to answer many questions about ways of input and output in Python.*

Q.1.1 **What will be the output of the following command(s) in Python?**

  (a) >>>print("Thank You God!")

  (b) >>>x="Pinky"

       >>>print("Believe in yourself ", x)

  (c) >>>print("3 raised to power 4 = ", 3**4)

  (d) >>>m=10

       >>>n=20

       >>>print(m, " + ", n, " = ", m+n)

  (e) >>>print(2+4, 6/3, 90*8)

  (f) >>> x=input()

         [12]

       >>>x

  (g) >>> x1= int(input('Enter an integer number'))

         [23]

       >>> x1

       Important terms: There is no explicit data type associated with a single variable. For example x=10 defines x to be an integer variable while x=9.5 defines it to be a floating variable. The character or string variables are defined using single or double quotes. The function input() function be default considers the input to be a string. We need to type cast these explicitly to integer using function int() or to floating-point using function float().

(h) >>> x=input()
   [12]
   >>> x1= int(input('Enter an integer number'))
   Enter an integer number [23]
   >>> x1+x

(i) >>> val=int(input('Enter a floating value'))
   Enter a floating value [23.7]

(j) >>> int1=float(input('Enter a floating value: '))
   Enter a floating value: [23]
   >>> int1

(k) >>>import string
   >>>for i in range(5):
   print(repr(i).rjust(5))

Important terms: There are many in-built functions provided in Python. These are defined using a module. One specific module contains all related functions. For example, the module math contains all functions related to mathematical functions. Similarly string module contains definition of all modules which can be performed with strings. In order to use the functions defined in a module, we need to import it using command

import *modulename*

(l) >>>"12".zfill(5)

(m) >>>print('{0:.3f}'.format(5.7416))

(n) >>> print('{0:.6f}'.format(5.9456))

(o) >>>print('{4:.3f}'.format(8.2496))

(p) >>>print('{0:9.3f}'.format(9.1011))

(q) >>> for x in ['Sunny', 'Monty']:
   print('hi "{} !"'.format(x))

(r) >>> print('{0:3d}, {2:6.1f}, {1:4d} '.format(1,2,3.0))

(s) >>>print('{0:3},{1:5},{2:6}'.format('Hello1','Bye2 ',3))

(t) >>> count = {'Unit': 1, 'Tenth': 10, 'Hundredth': 100}
   >>> for place, value in count.items():
   print('{0:10} ==> {1:10d}'.format(place, value))

Q.1.2 **State whether the statements given below are True or False:**

(i) The function input() takes an integer as input.

(ii) x,y = input() is as valid statement in Python.

(iii) We need to type cast in input value into an integer using function int().

(iv) We need to type cast in input value into a floating value using function float().

(v) We can input() a list of elements using a single input() function.

(vi) print(' {0} and {1}'. format('abcd', 24)) prints abcd as a string while 24 as an integer.

(vii) A number in the brackets refers to the position of the object passed into the **str.format()** method used in function print().

(viii) A function str.zfill() pads a numeric string on the right with zeros.

(ix) The result of '-5.24'.zfill(9) will be -000005.24

(x) '-5.24'.zfill(-10) fills zeroes in right making a total count of 10 digits.

ANSWERS

1.1

(a) print() function in Python takes a string argument in single quotes or double quotes and print it on the screen. So the output will be **Thank You God!**

(b) print() function in Python can take any number of arguments such as constant string, variable or an expression. In the given print() function, the two arguments are constant string and a string variable. So the value of string variable will be printed after the given string i.e. **Believe in Yourself Pinky**

(c) In given print() function, two arguments are passed, one is constant string and the other one is the arithmetic expression. The output will be constant string followed by the value of the arithmetic expression, i.e. **3 raised to power 4 = 81**.

(d) In given print() function, there are three types of arguments, constant strings, variables and an expression. The output will be constant strings, values of variables and evaluation of expression, i.e. **10 + 20 = 30**

(e) In given print() function, there are three arithmetic expressions. The output will be the result of their evaluations: **i.e. 6 2 720**

(f) In Python, input() function is used to input any value from user. The interpreter prompts at the console for input using a blinking vertical bar (|). The value entered is stored in variable on the left. By default, the value entered is stored as a string. So the output of value 12 entered as integer will be printed as string i.e. **'12'**.

(g) In Python, input() function is used to input any value from user. If it does not take any argument, the interpreter prompts at the console for input using a blinking vertical bar (|) without writing anything on the screen. But it prints the message on the screen if it is passed as an argument to input() function. The value entered is stored in variable on the left. By default, the value entered is stored as a string. So the function int() is used to type cast the string value into an integer. The output will be: **Enter an integer value:**

If value 23 entered as integer will be printed as **23**.

(h) The command is an arithmetic operator + which is taking an integer value and a string value which is not allowed in Python. An error message will be printed by the Python interpreter:

TypeError: unsupported operand type(s) for +: 'int' and 'str'

(i) The input() function is type casting the string value into an integer. It will print "Enter a floating value" because it is written in input() message, but when the user enters a floating-point value, an error is given:

ValueError: invalid literal for int() with base 10: '23.7'

(j) The value entered is stored as a floating-point value using type cast function float(). So value will be stored as **23.0** and printed on the screen.

(k) The values from 0 to 4 (not including 5) will be printed on each line right justified to 5 places.

0

1

2

3

4

(l) The output is printed as a string with total width 5 and zeroes filled on left **'00012'**.

(m) The output is formatted to three digits after decimal point. Since the value after decimal contains 4 digits, it has been rounded off : **5.742**

(n) The output is formatted to 6 digits after decimal point. Since the value after decimal contains 4 digits, zeroes have been added: **5.945600**

(o) Following error is reported because the index in the format string in print() should start from 0 instead of 4 as there is only 1 argument for printing

IndexError: tuple index out of range

(p) The output is justified to total 9 digits with three digits after decimal point. Since the value after decimal contains 4 digits, it has been rounded off:

9.101

(q) The two strings in the list are formatted according to the given format:

hi Sunny !

hi Monty !

(r) The output is formatted as follows: first integer argument justified to 3 digits (using 0:3d), second integer argument is justified to 4 digits (using 1:4d) and third floating point argument is justified to 6 places with one digit after decimal place (using 2:6.1f). Since the order given for printing is {0:3d}, {2:6.1f}, {1:4d}, so third value is printed after first value and then the second value:

1, 3.0, 2

(s) The output is formatted as follows: first integer argument justified to 3 digits (using 0:3), second integer argument is justified to 5 digits (using 1:5) and third integer argument is justified to 6 places (using 2:6). Since the order given for printing is {0:3}, {1:5}, {2:6}, the values are printed in the given order. For first argument only three spaces are reserved, but being a string, it will display the entire content, followed by second string left justified in 5 spaces and then integer value right justified to 6 places: **Hello1,Bye2 , 3**

(t) The output is formatted with place values left justified to 10 places and values right justified to 10 places: (printed in any order):

Unit   ==>   1

Hundredth ==>   100

Tenth   ==>   10

1.2

(i) False

By default, the function input() takes the value as a string.

(ii) False

Only one variable should be on the left side as we are taking only one input through function input()

(iii) True

   input() function takes the value as a string. Using function int() converts the value into an integer.

(iv) True

   input() function takes the value as a string. Using function float() converts the value into a floating value.

(v) False

   Only one value can be taken as input using function input(). The input() function is to be used in a loop for reading values in a list.

(vi) False

   We need to put {1d} in order to print the value as an integer.

(vii) True

(viii) False

   A function str.zfill() pads a numeric string on the left with zeros.

(ix) False

   The minus sign '-' will be counted in the total length 9.So the output will be -00005.24

(x) False

   It does not fill zeroes in the string and prints only the string as it is. This is because -10 in not a valid count of zeroes.

Chapter 2

Operators and Expressions

In this chapter you will be able to check how much you know about operators in Python. Please refer to Table 2 in Appendix for operators in Python and their precedence. B

Q.2.1 **State the output of executing the following expressions in Python:**

   (a) 27 + 8 * 2 - 6

   (b) 2 + 7 | 8 & 2

   (c) 3 - (5 + 4) * 2

   (d) 8 ^ 2 * 4 + 3

   (e) 9 * 6 - (4 | 6) + 5

   (f) (13 + 4) > (3 + 4)

   (g) (25 // 2 + 3.5) <= (7.5 + 20)

   (h) (40 and 50) or (0 or 30)

   (i) (40 and 50) and (0 or 20)

   (j) (not (200 | 120) and (30 & 20))

   (k) 2+3 * 5 & 7**2

   (l) 15 | 56*4+3-20

  (m) 20>>2>>3

   (n) 10<<3>>4

   (o) (12+20-10) and (34 & 3)

   (p) 45*90-8&4 | 5

   (q) 50^2>>8+20<<3

   (r) (40&5+10)<=(30+60 | 5)

   (s) (60^5) == (90^70)

    (t)   100>>5+90<<80

    (u) 9*10>>1-8

    (v)   1 in [1,2,3,4]

    (w) 1 not in [2,3,1,4]

    (x)   True is True

    (y)   (90 and 60 | 34) != (80 or 50 & 30)

    (z)   90-80+70-60+50*2

Q.2.2 **State whether each of the given statement is True/False:**

    i.   Bitwise operators have higher precedence than logical operators.

    ii.   ^ operator is a unary operator.

    iii. / and // operators give same output.

    iv. Logical operator 'and' returns True if all its operands are not False.

    v.   Logical operator 'or' returns True if any one of its operand is True.

    vi. Logical operator 'not' returns False if the operand is True.

    vii. Membership operator 'in' can be used with lists only.

    viii. Identity operator 'is' is used for testing whether the two objects are equal or not.

    ix. []==[] is True while [] is [] is False.

    x.   Multiplication by 2^n can be performed using left shift operator.

ANSWERS

2.1

a) 37

The highest precedence is of *. 8*2 gives 16. Since + and – have same precedence, these will be evaluated from left to right. 27+16 gives 43 and 43-6 gives 37. (Please see Appendix B)

b) 9

The highest precedence is of +. So 2+7 gives 9. Next precedence is of bitwise AND &. So 8&2 gives 0 (bitwise ANDing of 1000 and 0010). Next precedence is of |. So 9|0 gives 9 (bitwise ORing of 1001 and 0000).

c) -15

The highest precedence is of parenthesis (). So 5+4 gives 9. Next precedence is of * operator. So we get the value 9*2=18. Finally 3-18 gives -15.

d) 3

   Highest priority is of * operator. So 2*4 gives 8. Then, addition(+) of 8 and 3 is performed giving a value 11. Then XORing of 8 and 11 (8^11) gives 3 (1000 ^ 1011 = 0011).

e) 53

   Highest precedence is of (). So 4 | 6 (100 | 110) gives 6 (110). Then 9*6 gives 54. As – and + have same precedence, these are evaluated from left to right. 54-6 gives 48 and 48+5 is 53.

f) True

   The relational operator > returns True if the value on its left is greater than the value on its right. The value of the expression on its left is (13+4) i.e. 17 which is greater than (3+4) i.e. 7, value on its right.

g) True

   The relational operator <= returns True if the value on its left is less than or equal to the value on its right. The value of the expression on its left is (25 // 2 + 3.5) i.e. 12+3.5 = 15.5 which is less than (7.5 + 20) i.e. 27.5, value on its right.

h) 50

   In this expression, the operators used are logical 'and' and logical 'or'. Logical 'and' returns False if any one of the operand/expression is False or 0. Otherwise, it returns the value of last True operand or expression. Logical operator 'or' returns False if all the operands/expressions are False. Otherwise it returns the value of the first True operand/expression. In the given question, there are two expressions to operator or : (40 and 50) and (0 or 30). The expression (40 and 50) returns 50 because none of these is False and last value is 50. Since it is the first True value, the second operand is not evaluated and the value returned is 50.

i) 40

   In this expression, the operators used are logical 'and' and logical 'or'. Logical 'and' returns False if any one of the operand/expression is False or 0. Otherwise, it returns the value of last True operand or expression. Logical operator 'or' returns False if all the operands/expressions are False. Otherwise it returns the value of the first True operand/expression. In the given question, there are two expressions to operator and : (40 and 50) and (0 or 20). The expression (40 and 50) returns 50 because none of these is False and last value is 50. The expression (0 or 20) returns 20 since it is the first True value. The operator and returns the last value evaluated i.e. 20.

j) False

In this expression, the operators used are logical 'not', logical 'and', bitwise & and bitwise |. Logical 'and' returns False if any one of the operand/expression is False or 0. Otherwise, it returns the value of last True expression. Logical 'not' operator returns True if value of the operand/expression is False and returns False if the value of the operand/expression is True. Highest precedence is of 'not'. So (200 | 120) will be evaluated first which gives value 248. not(248) gives False. Since the first operand for and operator becomes False, it simply returns False without executing the next operand/expression.

k) 17

Highest priority is of ** operator. So 7**2 gives 49. 3*5 gives 15 and 2+15 gives 17. 17 & 49 gives 17.

l) 207

Highest priority is of * operator. So 56*4 gives 224. 224+3 gives 227. 227-20 gives 207. 15 | 207 gives 207.

m) 0

>> is evaluated from left to right. 20>>2 gives 5 and 5>>3 gives 0.

n) 5

>> and << have same priority, so are evaluated from left to right. 10<<3 gives 80 and 80>>4 gives 5

o) 2

There are two operands for operator 'and'. The expression (12+20-10) is evaluated from left to right, i.e. 32-10 i.e. 22. The second operand is 34&3 gives 2. Both operands are True and operand 'and' returns the last True expression.

p) 5

The operators '*' and '-' evaluated from left to right giving 4050-8 i.e. 4042. & and | are also evaluated from left to right. 4042&4 gives 0 and 0 | 5 gives 5.

q) 50

Highest precedence is of operator '+'. So 8+20 gives 28. Then >> and << are evaluated from left to right. 2>>28 gives 0 and 0<<3 gives 0. 50^0 gives 50.

r) True

The operator is <=. The two operands are evaluated and compared. (40&5+10) is evaluated as 5+10=15 followed by 40&15 which is 8.

(30+60 | 5) is evaluated as 30+60 i.e. 90 followed by 90 | 5 which is 95.

Since 8<=95, the operator returns True.

s) False

For the equality operator ==, two expressions to be evaluated are 60^5 which is 57 and (90^70) which is 28. Since these two are not equal, so the result is False.

t) 0

Highest precedence is of '+'. So 5+90 gives 95. >> and << are evaluated from left to right. 100>>95 gives 0 and 0<<80 gives 0.

u) 9*10 gives 90 and 1-8 gives -7. So 90>>-7 gives error as shift count cannot be negative.

So following message is shown:

Traceback (most recent call last):

File "<string>", line 1, in <module>

9*10>>1-8

ValueError: negative shift count

v) True

'in' operator checks whether the value is in the given list or not. Since 1 is present in the list, answer is True.

w) False

'not in' operator returns True if the value is not in the given list. Since 1 is present in the given list, so the answer is False.

x) True

'is' operator checks the identity of two variables. Since True is a unique object in Python, it returns True.

y) True

The two expressions for '!=' operators are (90 and 60|34) and (80 or 50 &30). 60|34 gives 62. 90 and 62 gives 62. Since 80 is True, operator 'or' returns 80. Since 62 !=80, answer is True.

z) 120

50*2 gives 100. '+' and '-' are evaluated from left to right. 90-80 gives 10, 10+70 gives 80, 80-60 gives 20 and 20+100 gives 120.

2.2

i. False

All logical operators have precedence lower than all bitwise operators. (refer to appendix on operator precedence)

ii. False

^ operator is binary bitwise XOR operator which performs the XOR of two operands. It returns 1 if the bits in two operands are different and returns 0 if bits in two operands are same.

   iii. False

a/b gives the actual value of the quotient on dividing a by b while a//b gives only integer part of the quotient on dividing a by b.

   iv. False

Logical operator 'and' returns the value of the last operand if all the operands are not False.

   v. False

Logical operator 'or' returns the value of the first operand which is not False.

   vi. True

Logical operator 'not' is a unary operator which returns the negation of the operand. If the value of the operand after evaluation is False, it returns True and if it is True, it returns False.

   vii. False

Membership operator 'in' can be used for testing whether a particular value in present in a list, string or tuple etc.

   viii. False

Identity operator 'is' is not used in Python to test whether the two objects are equal. It tests whether they are identical i.e. if the two variables refer to the same object.

Important terms: The equality operator '==' is used to check whether the values of two variables are equal or not.

   ix.   True

Important terms: An empty list [] is equal to anther empty list but these are not identical objects because they are not located at same place in memory.

   x. True

Important terms: One left shift inserts a 0 in right and hence the value gets multiplied by 2. So if a value is shifted left by n, it is multiplied by 2^n.

Chapter *3*

Decision Control Statements

In this chapter you will be asked questions based on if, if-else, if-elif statements.

Q.3.1 **What will be output of the following program?**

```
x=10
if x>10:
    x=x*5
    y=x-10
print(x,y)
```

Q.3.2 **What will be output of the following program?**

```
x=10
if x>=10:
    x=x*5
    y=x-10
print(x,y)
```

Q.3.3 **What will be output of the following program?**

```
value=1000
if value<10000:
    value-=50
print(value)
```

Q.3.4 **What will be output of the following program?**

```
x=10
if x>10:
    x*=5
    y=x-10
    if x>20:
```

```
        x*=2
        y=x+10
    print(x,y)
```

Q.3.5 What will be output of the following program?

```
x=10
if x>=10:
    x*=5
    y=x-10
    if x<20:
        x*=2
        y=x+10
print(x,y)
```

Q.3.6 What will be output of the following program?

```
x=10
if x>=10:
    x*=5
    y=x-10
    if x>20:
        x*=2
        y=x+10
print(x,y)
```

Q.3.7 What will be output of the following program?

```
v=300
if v%3==0:
    print(v, ' is divisible by 3')
else:
    print(v, ' is not divisible by 3')
```

Q.3.8 What will be output of the following program?

```
x=int(input('Enter an integer number: '))
if x>0:
    print (x, ' is a positive number')
elif x<0:
    print(x, 'is a negative number')
else:
    print('x is zero')
```

Q.3. 9 **What will be output of the following program?**

```
x=int(input('Enter a number between 1-7:'))
if x==7:
    print ('sunday')
elif x==6:
    print('monday')
elif x==5:
    print('tuesday')
elif x==4:
    print('wednesday')
elif x==3:
    print('thursday')
elif x==2:
    print('friday')
elif x==1:
    print('saturday')
else:
    print('invalid entry')
```

Q.3.10 **What will be output of the following program?**

```
v1 = -10
if v1:
    print ("1 - Got a true value", v1)
else:
    print ("1 - Got a false value", v1)
v2 = 0
if v2:
    print ("2 - Got a true value ", v2)
else:
    print ("2 - Got a false value ", v2)
v3 = 1000
if v3:
    print ("3 - Got a true value ", v3)
else:
    print ("3 - Got a false value ", v3)
```

Q.3.11 **What will be output of the following program?**

```
print("Input lengths of the triangle sides: ")
x = int(input("x: "))
```

```
y = int(input("y: "))
z = int(input("z: "))

if x == y == z:
    print("Equilateral triangle")
elif x != y != z:
    print("Scalene triangle")
else:
    print("isosceles triangle")
```

Q.3.12 What will be output of the following program?

```
a = float(input("Input the length of side1: "))
b = float(input("Input the length of side2: "))
c = float(input("Input the length of side3: "))

if (a < (b + c)) and (b < (a + c)) and (c < (a + b)):
    print("The triangle is valid.")
else:
    print("The triangle is not valid.")
```

Q.3.13 What will be output of the following program?

```
x = True
y = True
z = False
if not x or y:
    print (1)
elif not x or (not y and z):
    print (2)
elif (not x or y) or (y and x):
    print (3)
else:
    print (4)
```

Q.3.14 What will be output of the following program?

```
x = True
y = False
z = True
if not x or y:
    print (1)
elif not x or (not y and z):
```

```
        print (2)
elif (not x or y) or (y and x):
        print (3)
else:
        print (4)
```

Q.3.15 What will be output of the following program?

```
x = False
y = False
z = False
if x or y:
        print (1)
elif not x and (not y and z):
        print (2)
elif (not x or y) or (y and x):
        print (3)
else:
        print (4)
```

Q.3.16 State whether each of the following statement is True or False:

    i.   Only one condition can be given in one simple if statement.

    ii. We can write only if part of if statement without else part.

    iii. An if-elif ladder is used to test different values of same variable.

    iv. Any type of operators can be used in if conditions.

    v.   All conditions in if-elif ladder should be mutually exclusive.

    vi. The statement break is required to exit from each elif part.

    vii. The following if statement will print True:

```
if not 1:
        print('True')
else:
        print('False')
```

    viii. Consider the following if statement:

```
x,y=4,5
if x==4:
        print('x')
elif y==5:
        print('y')
else:
        print('nothing')
```

It is a good example for using if-elif ladder.

ix.   Any number of statements can be included in any block in if statement.

x.   The statements in else block are not executed if any of the condition in if-elif ladder is True.

ANSWERS

3.1 Nothing will be printed as the condition in if statement x>10 is False because the value of x is 10.

3.2 The value of x is 10 initially. The condition in if statement is True as x>=10, so the statements inside if statement will be executed. The value of x will be updated as 10*5 i.e. 50. Variable y has no value initially. It is assigned the value 50-10 i.e. 40. The output will be 50,40.

3.3 The initial value of the variable value is 1000. The condition in if statement is True because value<10000. Inside the if body, value is decremented by 50 i.e. 1000-50 which gives the output as 950.

3.4 The condition in if statement is not True because value of x is 10 which is not greater than 10. So the statements in if body are not executed.
The print statement is executed which contains an undefined variable y. The output will be: NameError: name 'y' is not defined.

3.5 The condition in if statement is True as x>=10. The value of x is updated as 10*5 i.e. 50. Variable y is assigned value 50-10 i.e. 40. The condition in nested if statement is False because value of x is not less than 20. So the value of x as 50 and value of y as 40 is printed. The output is 50,40.

3.6 The condition in if statement is True as x>=10. The value of x is updated as 10*5 i.e. 50. Variable y is assigned value 50-10 i.e. 40. The condition in nested if statement is True because value of x is greater than 20. So the value of x is updated as 50*2 i.e. 100 and value of y is updated as x+10 i.e. 110 and printed. The output is 100,110.

3.7 The condition in if statement is True. The output will be: **300 is divisible by 3**.

3.8 The program will ask the user to input an integer number and stores it in variable x. Suppose value entered is 34. It checks the value of x. If it is greater than 0, it prints 34 is a positive number and exits the if statement. If the value entered for x is -8, the condition in if statement fails and it checks condition in elif statement which is True. So it prints -8 is a negative number and exits the if statement. If the value entered is neither >0 nor <0, it means it is zero. So the else part of if is executed and x is zero is printed on screen.

3.9 The program will ask the user to enter a number between 1 and 7 and stores in variable x. It has if-elif ladder. It prints the day of the week according to the number entered. If x is 7, it prints Sunday and exits the if-elif ladder. If it is other than 7 but greater than or equal to 1, it prints corresponding day of the week and exits the if-elif ladder. If the value of x is not between 1 and 7(both inclusive), it matches with none of the conditions in the if-elif ladder, so the control reaches in else block and prints Invalid entry.

3.10 There are three if-else statements in the program. Any value other than 0 is treated as True and value 0 is treated as False. The output will be:

1 - Got a true value -10

2 - Got a false value 0

3 - Got a true value 1000

3.11 The given Python program checks whether a triangle is equilateral, isosceles or scalene. An equilateral triangle is a triangle in which all three sides x,y,z are equal. A scalene triangle is a triangle that has three unequal sides. An isosceles triangle is a triangle with (at least) two equal sides.

For input: x=10, y=10, z=10

The output will be:

"Equilateral triangle"

3.12 The given Python function takes as input three sides of a triangle and prints whether the triangle is valid or not. A triangle is valid if (a < (b + c)) and (b < (a + c)) and (c < (a + b)).

For input:

a=20 b=30 c=10

The output will be:

"The triangle is valid."

3.13 Here x, y and z are Boolean variables with values True, True and False respectively. First condition in if statement is True (not x or y). So the statement in the first if is executed.

The output is: **1**

3.14 Here x, y and z are Boolean variables with values True, False and True respectively. First condition in if statement is False (not x or y). but second condition is True (not x or (not y and z)). So the statement in the first elif is executed.

The output is: **2**

3.15 Here x, y and z are Boolean variables with values False, False and False respectively. First condition in if statement is False (x or y). Second condition is also False (not x and (not y and z)). Third condition is True ((not x or y) or (y and x)). So the statement in the this elif is executed. The output is: **3**

3.16 i.   **False**

There can be more than one conditions in one simple if statement but these should be combined using logical operators forming a compound condition. For example a>8 and b%3.

ii.   True

There are situations where we need to work only when certain condition is True and nothing if that is False. So there is no need for else part.

iii. True
iv.   True

Though the value in if statement should return either True or False, but a value 0 is treated as False while any value other than 0 is treated as True. So any type of operator can be used as condition in if statement. For example, following if statement will print **It is non-zero** since 8+9 is a True value.

if 8+9:

    print('It is non zero')

v.   True

This is because only one part of if statement is executed based on certain True condition and then it exits the if statement.

vi.   False

The if-elif ladder exits immediately after it executes the statements without the use of break statement.

vii. False

1 is True and so 'not 1' will return False. Hence the statement in the else part will be executed and 'False' will be printed.

viii. False

Since x is 4 and y is 5, so both x and y should be printed. Using these in if-elif ladder does not serve the purpose. So in if-elif ladder mutually exclusive values of same variables should be considered.

ix.   True
x.   True

Important terms: The statements in the else part are executed only of all conditions in all if –elif statements are False.

Chapter 4

Loops

> *In this chapter you will be asked questions about for loop and while loop in Python.*

Q.4.1 **State what will be the output of the following programs?**

(a) ```
for i in range(4):
    print(i)
```

(b) ```
for i in range(4,7):
        print(i)
```

(c) ```
for i in range(14,28,4):
        print(i)
```

(d) ```
for i in range(24,18,-3):
        print(i)
```

(e) ```
sum=0
for i in range(20,10,-2):
    sum+=i
print(sum)
```

(f) ```
sum=0
for i in range(10,20,2):
    sum+=i
print(sum)
```

(g) ```
sum=0
for i in range(10,20,-2):
    sum+=i
print(sum)
```
```

(h)
```
i=10
for i in range(5):
    print(i)
    i = i+3
    print(i)
```

(i)
```
p=1
n=int(input('enter a number'))
for i in range(1,n+1):
    p*=i
print(n, '! = ', p)
```

(j)
```
i=0
while i<=9:
    if i%3==0:
        print(i)
    i=i+1
print("Out of loop")
```

(k)
```
i=0
while i>=9:
    if i%3==0:
        print(i)
    i=i+1
print("Out of loop")
```

(l)
```
i=1
sum_e,sum_o=0,0
while i<=10:
    if i%2==0:
        sum_e+=i
    else:
        sum_o+=i
    i=i+1
print("Sum of even numbers: ", sum_e)
print("Sum of odd numbers: ", sum_o)
```

(m)
```
i=1
sum_e=0
sum_o=0
while i<=5:
    n=int(input())
```

```
    if n%2==0:
        sum_e+=n
    else:
        sum_o+=n
    i=i+1
print("Sum of even numbers: ", sum_e)
print("Sum of odd numbers: ", sum_o)
```

(n)
```
for i in range(2):
    for j in range(3):
        print(i,j)
```

(o)
```
i,j=0,0
while i<2:
    while j<3:
        print(i,j)
        i+=1
        j+=1
```

(p)
```
for i in range(2):
sum_r=0
for j in range(3):
    n = int(input('enter'))
    sum_r+=n
print(sum_r)
```

(q)
```
sum=0
for i in range(2):
    for j in range(3):
        n = int(input('enter'))
        sum+=n
print(sum)
```

(r)
```
z=10
w=-10
while(z<50):
    if (z>0 and w<0):
        print(z**2, w**3)
        z = z+10
        w=w+10
```

(s)
```
z,w=10,-10
while(z<50):
```

```
        if (z>0 or w<0):
            print(z**2, w**3)
            z = z+10
            w=w+10
```

(t)   for k in range(3, 21, 3):
```
        if k%5==0:
            break
        print(k)
```

(u)   for k in range(3, 21, 3):
```
        if k%5==0:
            continue
        print(k)
```

Q. 4.2 State whether each of the following statement is True or False :

  i.   We cannot nest one for loop inside another while loop.

 ii.   Using a break statement causes the outermost loop to exit.

iii.   A continue statement skips the statements after it in the current iteration of the loop.

 iv.   The result of condition in for or while loop is True or False.

  v.   Consider the loop below:
```
        i=0
        sum=0
        while i>90:
            if i%10==0:
                sum=sum+i
            i=i+5
        print("Sum = ", sum)
```

The output will be 360.

 vi.   Consider the loop below:
```
        i=0
        sum=0
        while i<90:
```

```
        if i%10==0:
            sum=sum+i
        i=i+5
    print("Sum = ", sum)
```

The output will be 360.

vii. n1 = [0 for i in range(5)] creates a list n1 of numbers from 0 to 5.

viii. Consider the code below:

```
    l=[1,2,3,45,26]
    max=0
    for i in l:
        if i>max:
            max=i
    print(max)
```

The output will be 45

ix. By default, the for loop iteration starts from 1.

x. The default update is increment by 1 in for loop.

ANSWERS

4.1

a) In the given for loop, the value of variable i will vary from 0 to 3. So the output will be:

    0
    1
    2
    3

b) In the given for loop, the value of variable i will vary from 4 to 6. So the output will be:

    4
    5
    6

c) In the given for loop, the value of variable i will vary from 14 to 27 with an increment of 4. So the output will be:

14
18
22
26

d) In the given for loop, the value of variable i will vary from 24 to 19 with a decrement of 3. So the output will be:

24
21

e) In the given for loop, the value of variable i will vary from 20 to 11 with a decrement of 2. The values of i will be 20,18,16,14 and12. Each value of i will be added to variable sum in each iteration.

So the output will be: 20+18+16+14+12 i.e. **80**.

f) In the given for loop, the value of variable i will vary from 10 to 18 with an increment of 2. The values of i will be 10,12,14,16 and18. Each value of i will be added to variable sum in each iteration.

So the output will be: 10+12+14+16+18 i.e. **70**.

g) The value of sum will not be incremented as the update value is -2. The output will be: **0**

Important term: Please check the initial value and terminating value and set update value accordingly

h) The given for loop is varying the value of i from 0 to 4. The print statement prints the current value of i, increments it by 3 and prints it. The value of variable i is unaffected in the loop.

The output will be:
0
3
1
4
2
5
3
6
4
7

Important term: The value of the index variable executes separately as defined in the definition of the for loop

i) This given loop inputs an integer number and prints its factorial(!) where n! = n*(n-1)*(n-2)*...*3*2*1. If input is 5, the output will be:

5! = 120

j) The given while loop executes till the value of i is less than or equal to 9. It is incrementing it by 1 inside the while loop. If it is divisible by 3, it is printed. The loop exits when value of i becomes 10. Then the print statement after the while loop is executed.

The output will be:

0

3

6

9

Out of loop

k) In the given loop, the condition in while is False. So no statement in the loop will be executed. So the output will be:

Out of loop

l) In the given loop, value of variable i varies from 1 to 10. The even numbers are added in variable sum_e and the odd numbers are added in variable sum_o. The output will be:

Sum of even numbers: 30

Sum of odd numbers: 25

m) The given loop inputs 5 integer values from user. The even values are added in variable sum_e and the odd values are added in variable sum_o. If the input is:

12

12

45

34

67

The output will be:

Sum of even numbers: 58

Sum of odd numbers: 112

n) The given for loop is a nested for loop. Variable i varies from 0 to 1 and variable j in inner loop varies from 0 to 2. So the output will be:

0 0

0 1

0 2

1 0
1 1
1 2

o) Given loop is a nested while loop. Variable i varies from 0 to 1 and variable j in inner loop varies from 0 to 2. So the output will be:

0 0
0 1
0 2
1 0
1 1
1 2

p) The given nested for loop input values in a 2D matrix with 2 rows and 3 columns. It stores the sum of elements in each row in variable sum_r. For the following matrix:

1 2 4
4 5 6

The output will be:

7
15

Important term: A 2 Dimensional matrix is stored row-wise in the memory.

q) The given nested for loop reads elements of a 2D matrix of order 2X3. The sum of all elements in the matrix is stored in variable sum. For the following matrix:

1 2 3
4 5 6

The output will be: **21**

r) In the given while loop, variables z and w are initialized to 10 and -10 respectively. Condition in if statement is True only once. The output will be:

100 -1000

s) In the given while loop, variables z and w are initialized to 10 and -10 respectively. Condition in if statement is True 4 times. The output will be:

100 -1000

400 0

900 1000

1600 8000

t) In the given for loop, variable k varies from 3 to 20 with an increment of 3. If the value of k is divisible by 5, the loop exits, else the value of k is printed.

The output will be:

3

6

9

12

u) In the given for loop, variable k varies from 3 to 20 with an increment of 3. If the value of k is divisible by 5, the loop continues to next iteration, else the value of k is printed.

The output will be:

3

6

9

12

18

4.2

i. False

It can be done.

ii. False

Using a break statement causes the innermost loop to exit.

iii. True

iv. True

v. False

This is because the condition i>90 is False. So no statement inside the while loop
is executed.

Sum = 0

vi. True

This is because the condition i<90 is True. So the values of i which are divisible by 10 will be added to sum.

Sum = 10+20+30+40+50+60+70+80 = 360

vii. False

It creates a list n1 of 5 0's i.e. [0,0,0,0,0].

viii. True

for loop assigns the largest value to variable max.

ix. False

By default, iteration in for loop starts from 0.

x. True

Functions

> In this chapter you will be able to check how much you
> know about defining new functions and using existing
> ones in Python.

Q.5.1 **State error(s), if any, in the following function defintions:**

(a) def welcome()
    print('Welcome to Programming in Python!')

(b) def main():
    print 'Error finding in Python!'

(c) def prn:
    print('Syntax Error in Python!')

(d) def main():
    print('Corrections for Errors in Python!)

(e) def prnline():
    print("Be a Pythonist!')

(f) def indent():
    print("Sarah Beth is a swimming champion! ")

(g) def Pyn():
    print("Be Positive! ")

(h) def 1Pyn():
    print("Be Simple! ")

(i) def break():
    print("Simple is better than complex! ")

(j) def pep8(x y):
         print("Beautiful is better than ugly! ")

Q.5.2 State the task/function performed by each of the following functions in Python:

(a) def f1(a,b,c):
         return (a+b+c)
     f1(20,40,60)

(b) def f2(x,y,z):
         return (x+y+z)//3
     f2(20,41,60)

(c) def f3(m,n):
         if m>=n:
             print(m)
         else:
             print(n)
     f3(40,10)

(d) def f4(n):
         for i in range(1,n+1):
             print(i)
     f4(5)

(e) def f5(a,b):
         while b:
             a,b = b, a%b
         print (a)
     f5(300,500)

(f) def f6(n):
         sum = 0
         for x in range(1, n):
             if n % x == 0:
                 sum += x
         return sum == n
     print(f6(6))

(g) def f7():

```
def f7():
    for v in range(8):
        if v % 3 == 0 and v % 5 == 0:
            print("PythonPy")
            continue
        elif v % 3 == 0:
            print("Python3")
            continue
        elif v % 5 == 0:
            print("Python5")
            continue
        print(v)
f7()
```

(h) def f8(n):

```
def f8(n):
    m = n
    sum = 0
    while m!=0:
        x = m%10
        sum = sum + x**3
        m = m//10
    if sum == n:
        print(n, " is an Armstrong number")
    else:
        print(n, " is not an Armstrong number")
f8(153)
f8(125)
```

(i) def f9(n,x):

```
def f9(n,x):
    i=2
    j=2
    t=1
    sum = 0
    while t<=n:
        sum = sum + x**i * (-1)**j
        print(sum)
        i = i+2
        j = j+1
        t = t+1
    print(sum)
f9(3,2)
```

(j) def f10(n):
```
    i =1
    while i<=10:
        print(i , "*", n, "=", n*i)
        i=i+1
f10(5)
```

(k) def f11(n):
```
    if n == 2:
        print(n, ' is a prime number')
    elif n%2 == 0:
        print(n, ' is not a prime number')
    else:
        for i in range(3, int(n/2) , 2):
            if n % i == 0:
                print(n, 'is not a prime number')
                break
        print(n, ' is a prime number')
f11(29)
```

(l) def f12(n):
```
    sum = 0
    while n != 0:
        k = n % 10
        sum = sum + k
        k = int(n / 10)
        n = k
    print("Sum of digits: ", sum)
f12(123)
```

(m) def f13():
```
    k = 1
    sum = 0
    multi = 1
    print("Enter a number: ")
    n = int(input())
    print("Enter the number of digits: ")
    nd = int(input())
    print("Reversed Number : ")
    while k <= nd:
        k1 = n % 10
```

```
            print(k1)
            sum = sum + k1
            n = int(n / 10)
            k = k + 1
        print("Sum of digits: ", sum)
    f13()
```

(n) def f14(n):
```
        count = 0
        print('Numbers from 1 to n not divisible by 2,3 and 5')
        for num in range(n+1):
            if num%2 != 0 and num%3!=0 and num%5!=0:
                print( num)
                count = count + 1;
        print('Total numbers: ', count )
```

f14(30)

(o) def f15(year):
```
        if year % 4 == 0:
            if year % 100 == 0:
                if year % 400 == 0:
                    print(year, ' is a leap year')
                else:
                    print(year, ' is not a leap year')
            else:
                print(year, ' is a leap year')
        else:
            print(year, ' is not a leap year')
    f15(400)
    f15(1981)
```

ANSWERS

5.1

a) Whenever a function is defined using def, a colon(:) is placed after the name of the function . So an invalid syntax will be reported in Python IDLE here as Colon (:) is missing after welcome().
Correct statement:
def welcome() :

Important terms: A function is defined using the syntax

def function_name(arg1, arg2...):
Function-body

The function name should not be a keyword in Python, it can contain numbers and underscore but should not contain space and it should start with small letter.

b) The arguments to a print function are to be put inside a pair of parentheses().So an invalid syntax will be reported in Python IDLE : "Missing parentheses in call to 'print' " here as set of parenthesis () are missing for print statement.

Correct statement:
print ('Error finding in Python!')

c) Every function name should include arguments inside a pair of parentheses (). Without any arguments an empty parentheses should be there to indicate that the variable name is name of a function. So an invalid syntax will be reported in Python IDLE here as set of parenthesis () are missing after function name prn.

Correct statement:
def prn():

d) The string to be printed using print function should be included in a pair of either single quotation marks or double quotation marks. So an invalid syntax will be reported in Python IDLE here as closing single quote (') missing in print statement.

Correct statement:
print ('Corrections for Errors in Python!')

e) The string to printed using print function should be included in a pair of either single quotation marks or double quotation marks. But the two types of quotation marks cannot be mixed together. So a syntax error will be reported in Python IDLE : SyntaxError: "EOL while scanning string literal" here as we cannot mix the two types of quotation marks in print statement.

Correct statement:
print("Be a Pythonist! ") or
print('Be a Pythonist!')

f) Syntax error will be reported in Python IDLE : "expected an indented block" here as the function body should be indented in next line by 4 spaces or a tab.

Correct statement:

def indent():

    print("Sarah Beth is a swimming champion")

Important terms: In Python, indentation is very important and essential for every statement. All the statements in the body of the function should be indented.

g) A function name in Python should start with a small letter or underscore. However no syntax error will be reported.
Output: The contents of the print() will be printed on the screen. Be Positive!

h) A function name in Python should start with a small letter or underscore. So an invalid syntax error will be reported as a function name cannot start with a numeric.

Correct statement:

def pyn():

i) A function name in Python cannot be a keyword. 'break' is a keyword which is used for breaking out of the current loop. So an invalid syntax error will be reported as a function name cannot be a reserve keyword.

Correct statement:

def breakForFun():

or

def break1():

j) The arguments passed in a function should be separated by a comma. So an invalid syntax will be reported as there should be a comma between two arguments.

Correct statement:

def pep8(x, y):

5.2

a) Function f1 returns the sum of three numbers passed as arguments. The output will be:

120

b) Function f2 returns the average of three numbers passed as arguments. It returns the integer part of the average. The output will be:

40

c) Function f3 returns the larger of the two numbers passed as arguments. The output will be:

40

d) Function f4 prints numbers from range 1 to n (passed as argument). The output will be:

1

2

3

4

5

e) Function f5 finds the GCD of given two numbers. So for 300 and 500, the output is 100.

f) Function f6 checks whether the given number is a perfect number or not. For 6 it is True, so answer will be True.

g) For multiples of three, function f7 prints "Python3" instead of the number and for the multiples of five the function prints "Python5". For numbers which are multiples of both three and five the function prints "PythonPy". The output will be:

1

2

Python3

4

Python5

Python3

7

h) Function f8 checks whether a number entered by the users is an Armstrong number or not. A number is Armstrong if it is equal to the sum of the cubes of its digits. The output will be:

153 is an Armstrong number as $153 = 1^3+5^3+3^3$.

125 is not an Armstrong number because $125 \neq 1^3+2^3+5^3$.

i) Function f9 finds the sum of the series: $x^2-x^4+x^6-x^8+.....$upto n terms. Here n is 3 and x is 2. So it prints the sum of the series $2^2-2^4+2^6$. The output will be:

-4

12

52

52

j) Function f10 prints the table of the given number(5) here. The output will be:

$1 * 5 = 5$

$2 * 5 = 10$

$3 * 5 = 15$

$4 * 5 = 20$

$5 * 5 = 25$

$6 * 5 = 30$

$7 * 5 = 35$

$8 * 5 = 40$

$9 * 5 = 45$

$10 * 5 = 50$

k) Function f11 prints whether the given number is prime or not. A number is prime if it is not divisible by any number other than 1 and number itself. For 29, the output will be :

29 is a prime number

l) Function f12 prints the sum of the digits of the given number. For 6, the output will be:

Sum of digits: 6

m) Function f13 prints the integer entered in reverse. For example, if input is 147 and 3(for number of digits), the output will be:

Reversed Number :

7

4

1

Sum of digits: 12

n) Function f14 prints numbers from 1 to n which are not divisible by 2,3 and 5. The output will be:

Numbers from 1 to n not divisible by 2,3 and 5

1

7

11

13

17

19

23

29

Total numbers: 8

o) The function prints whether the given year is a leap year or not. The output will be:

400 is a leap year

1981 is not a leap year

Lists

In this chapter you will be able to check how much you know about lists in Python.

6.1 What will be the output of the following commands?

```
>>> mywords = ['Krishna', 'Rameshwar Dass', 'Usha', 'Ramesh']
>>> for w in mywords:
        print(w,)
```

6.2 What will be the output of the following commands?

```
>>> goodwords = ['positive thinking', 'faith','hard work']
>>> print(len(goodwords))
```

6.3 What will be the output of the following commands?

```
>>> success=['Hard work','Patience','Hope','Dreaming Big']
>>> list(enumerate(success))
```

6.4 What will be the output of the following commands?

```
>>> good_luck = ['Destiny', 'Opportunities', 'Devotion']
>>> list(enumerate(good_luck, start = 1))
```

6.5 What will be the output of the following commands?

```
>>> x = [1,2,3]
>>> x = x + [9,10]
>>> x
```

6.6 What will be the output of the following commands?

```
>>> list1 = [5,50,'Five Hundred']
```

```
>>> list2 = list(list1)
>>> list2
```

6.7 **Consider the final list list2 in Q.6.6, what will be the output of the following commands?**

```
>>> list2[2:3] = [500, 5000]
>>> list2
```

6.8 **What will be the output of the following commands?**

```
>>> week = ['sun', 'mon', 'tue', 'wed', 'feb', 'thu', 'fri', 'sat']
>>> week[4:5] = []
>>> week
```

6.9 **Consider the final list week in Q. 6.8, what will be the output of the following commands?**

```
>>> week[5] = []
>>> week
```

6.10 **What will be the output of the following commands?**

```
>>> hobbies = ['Painting', 'Creative Writing', 'Reading']
>>> hobbies[:] = []
>>> hobbies
```

6.11 **What will be the output of the following commands?**

```
>>> list1= [10,20,30,4,4]
>>> print(list1.count(4))
```

6.12 **What will be the output of the following commands?**

```
>>> list1 = []
>>> if not list1:
        print("List is empty")
```

6.13 **What will be the output of the following program?**

```
>>> list1 = [14,19, 20, 21]
>>> list1.remove(19)
>>> list1
```

6.14 **What will be the output of the following commands?**

```
>>> list1=[22,33]
>>> list2= [11,22,13]
>>> print(list1<list2)
```

6.15 **What will be the output of the following commands?**

```
>>> m = [[x, y] for x in range(0, 3) for y in range(0, 4)]
>>> print(m)
```

6.16 **What will be the output of the following commands?**

```
>>> list1=[10,20]
>>> n= 30
>>> list1.insert(1,n)
>>> list1
```

6.17 **What will be the output of the following commands?**

```
>>> num=[10,20]

>>> n= 30
>>> num.append(n)
>>> m=40
>>> num.append(m)
>>> print(num)
```

6.18 **What will be the output of the following commands?**

```
>>> num=[100,200]
>>> num.extend([30,40,50])

>>> num
```

6.19 **What will be the output of the following commands?**

```
>>> num=[1,2,3,4,5]
>>> num.pop()
>>> num
>>> num.pop(1)
>>> num
```

6.20 **What will be the output of the following commands?**

```
>>> pow2 = [2 ** x for x in range(10) if x %2 ==0]
>>> print(pow2)
```

Q. **Select the appropriate answer for the following questions:**

6.21 **Which of the following method(s) can be used to add an item to the end of a given list?**

a) append( )
b) insert( )
c) extend( )
d) All of these

6.22 Which of the following method can be used to add more than one items to a given list?

a) append( )
b) insert( )
c) extend( )
d) All of these

6.23 Which of the following method can be used to add an item at any position in a given list?

a) append( )
b) insert( )
c) extend( )
d) All of these

6.24 Which of the following method returns the element removed from a given position in the list?

a) remove( )
b) pop( )
c) clear( )
d) All of these

6.25 Which of the following method is used to remove all elements from a given list?

a) remove( )
b) clear( )
c) pop( )
d) All of the above

6.26 Which item is removed from the list in case the index is not specified in pop( ) method?

a) first
b) last
c) current
d) All

6.27 Which of the following statement/method is used to remove an item from a list by giving its value?

    a) pop( )

    b) remove

    c) clear( )

    d) None of these

6.28 Which of the following statement/method is used to remove an item from a list using index value?

    a) pop( )

    b) del

    c) clear( )

    d) None of these

6.29 What is the return type of methods sort( ), remove( ) and insert( )?

    a) None

    b) a list

    c) an item

    d) Any of these

6.30 Is list a mutable data structure in Python? State True or False.

    a) True

    b) False

ANSWERS

6.1 The for loop prints each element of the list. Since comma(,) is put in print () function, all elements will be printed on same line:

Krishna, Rameshwar Dass, Usha, Ramesh

6.2 len() function returns the total number of elements in the given list:

[3]

6.3 enumerate() function lists the elements of the list along with index number which is 0 by default. The output is:

[(0, 'Hard work'), (1, 'Patience'), (2, 'Hope'), (3, 'Dreaming Big')]

6.4 enumerate() function lists the elements of the list along with index number which is 0 by default. Using the starting value with an argument start, the index of all elements in the list can be changed:

[(1, 'Destiny'), (2, 'Opportunities'), (3, 'Devotion')]

6.5 The + operator works for lists as concatenation operator and returns a list which is composed of first list followed by second list:

[1, 2, 3, 9, 10]

6.6 The list() function is used to create a new list be copying the contents of the list passed as argument. Note that one list can contain any type

The output is: [5, 50, 'Five Hundred']

6.7 The elements of a list are indexed starting from 0. Here the value 'Five Hundred' exists at list2[2]. The command given replaces this with new integer value 500 and also adds at the same time a new value 5000 at index list2[3]. The output is:

[5, 50, 500, 5000]

6.8 The list elements at index 4 till 5 (not including 5) will be deleted from the list. The rest of the elements will be moved forward in the list by the number of elements deleted. The output is:

['sun', 'mon', 'tue', 'wed', 'thu', 'fri', 'sat']

6.9 Replacing a particular element in a list deletes that from the list but empty list [] is there to indicate the deletion. The output is:

[' sun', 'mon', 'tue', 'wed', 'thu', [], 'sat']

6.10 Using [:] in the list as an index indicates the entire list. As the command replaces each element with a [], the entire list hobbies is empty, []

6.11 count() function returns the count of the given element in the given list. As 4 appears 2 times in the list given, the output will be 2.

6.12 The list variable list1 is initialized to empty []. The if condition uses not operator and prints "List is empty" because not list1 is True because list1 is False.

The output will be List is empty

6.13 remove() function deletes the value 19 from given list [14,19,20,21]

The output will be:

[14,20,21]

6.14 list1<list2 returns True if all the elements of list1 are less than elements of list2 which is not True here

The output will be: False

6.15 It is a command to create a two dimensional list where x is varying from 0 to 3 and y is varying from 0 to 3

The output will be the list:

[[0, 0], [0, 1], [0, 2], [0, 3], [1, 0], [1, 1], [1, 2], [1, 3], [2, 0], [2, 1], [2, 2], [2, 3]]

6.16 Here the program inserts number n=30 at index 1 i.e. second position in given list [10,20].

The output will be : **[10,30,20]**

6.17 Here the program inserts number n=30 at the end of the given list [10,20]. The list becomes [10,20,30]. Then m=40 is inserted at the end of this list.

The output will be: **[10,20, 30, 40]**

6.18 The given list [100,200] will be extended by inserting all values at the end of the list.

The output will be: **[100,200,30,40,50]**

6.19 pop() function removes and returns the last element of the given list [1,2,3,4,5]

The output will be: **5** and the list will be **[1,2,3,4]**.

pop(1) removes and returns the second element at index 1 in the list [1,2,3,4]

The output will be: **2** and the list will be **[1,3,4]**

6.20 The list comprehension will create a list of 2_x where x varies from 0 to 9 and x is even.

The output will be:

[$2_0, 2_2, 2_4, 2_8$] i.e. [1, 4, 16, 64, 256]

6.21 a and c

6.22 c

6.23 b

6.24 b

6.25 b

6.26 b

6.27 b

6.28 a

6.29 a

6.30 a

Strings

> In this chapter you will be able to check how much you know string handling in Python.

Q.7.1 **What will be the output of the following commands?**

(a) >>> 'hello'+'world'

(b) >>> 3*'hi'+2*'Usha'

(c) >>> for c in "Gariyasi" :
               print(c)

(d) >>> for ch in " i love my Mammy and Papa":
               print(ch,)

(e) >>> weekend="satsun"

      >>> print(weekend[3:6])

(f) >>> name = "Guido van Rossum"
      >>> print(name[0]+name[:6])

(g) >>> name = "Bhavica Bansal"
      >>> print(name[-5])

(h) >>> name = "Sujoy Bansal"
      >>>print(name[:-5])

(i) >>> name = "Sh. Ramesh Chand Goel"
      >>> print(name[:])

(j) >>> len("Prakriti ! ")

(k) >>> s= "Amit is elder to Sandeep"
     >>> print(s.count('e'))

(l) >>>import string
     >>>s = "Bennett University"
     >>>str. find(s, 'i')

(m) >>> import string
     >>> str.join(" Bennett Colman and Co. Ltd. ", "TOI")

(n) >>> eval("47.5 + 27.5")

(o) def comparison(word):
         if word == 'Apple' :
             print('Your word is Apple')
     elif word < 'Apple' :
         print('Your word', word, ', comes before Apple')
     else:
         print('Your word', word, ', comes after Apple')
     >>> comparison('Banana')

(p) >>>print('"It isn't true," Vishal said.')
     >>>print('"It isn\'t true," Vishal said.')

(q) >>> import string
     >>> s = "deepak is very loving and caring!"
     >>> str.capitalize(s)

(r) >>> import string
     >>> s = "Gariyasi Prakriti Anrav Ayushi Ishaan"
     >>> str.lower(s)

(s) >>> import string
     >>> str.split("Krishna Ajay Monika")

(t) >>> import string
     >>> s = "I am proud to be Indian"
     >>> str.replace(s,'Indian', 'Hindustani')

(u) >>>print("Did you smile today ?". split())

(v)
```python
def odd_values_string(str):
    result = ""
    for i in range(len(str)):
        if i % 2 == 0:
            result = result + str[i]
    return result

print(odd_values_string('a1b2c3d4e5f6g7h8i9'))
```

(w)
```python
name= "John Parera"
n=name.split()
n.insert(1, "Peter")
print(" ".join(n))
```

(x)
```python
n="cock-bear-seal-cow"
items=n.split('-')
items.sort()
print('-'.join(items))
```

(y)
```python
month = input("Input the month(January, February...): ")
day = int(input("Input the day: "))

if month in ('January', 'February', 'March'):
        season = 'winter'
elif month in ('April', 'May', 'June'):
        season = 'spring'
elif month in ('July', 'August', 'September'):
        season = 'summer'
else:
        season = 'autumn'

if (month == 'March') and (day > 19):
        season = 'spring'
elif (month == 'June') and (day > 20):
        season = 'summer'
elif (month == 'September') and (day > 21):
        season = 'autumn'
elif (month == 'December') and (day > 20):
```

```
        season = 'winter'

    print("Season is", season)

(z) def add_string(str1):
        if str1[-3:] == 'ing':
            str1 = str1
        else:
            str1 += 'ing'
        return str1

    print(add_string('fly'))

    print(add_string('cry'))

    print(add_string('string'))
```

Q.7.2 **State True/False for the following statements:**

    i. Any integer or floating-point value can be converted into a string using function str().

    ii. Strings can be indexed using negative and positive numbers.

    iii. String slicing using s[x:y] returns a sub-string from s[x] to s[y].

    iv. String slicing using s[:i] returns a sub-string from beginning to s[i].

    v. String slicing using s[i:] returns a sub-string from s[i] till end.

    vi. String slicing using s[-2:] returns characters from the second-last to the end of the string.

    vii. Strings in Python are mutable.

    viii. If word is defined as a string of length 10, then word[2:] = 'hello' is a valid statement in Python.

    ix. If word = "String", then 'J' + word[1:] is a valid statement.

    x. If w = "String", then statement w[:3] + 'doc' is an invalid statement.

ANSWERS

7.1

a) Concatenation of strings takes place using '+' operator :

   'helloworld'

b) Concatenation (using '+' operator) along with repetition of strings (using '*' operator) takes place:

   'hihihiUshaUsha'

c) Each character of the string is printed on a new line:

   G

   a

   r

   i

   y

   a

   s

   i

d) Each character of the string is printed on the same line due to , in the end of print() function:

   i love my Mammy and Papa

e) String slicing takes place. The characters starting at index 3 till 5 (not including 6) are printed on the screen:

   sun

f) Concatenation of strings takes place using '+' operator where first is character at index 0 from string variable name followed by first 6 characters of string variable name:

   GGuido

g) String slicing takes place. 5th Character from last of string variable name is printed on the screen:

   a

h) String slicing takes place. All characters except last 5 characters in string variable name are printed on the screen:

   Sujoy B

i) String slicing takes place. All characters in string variable name are printed on the screen:

Sh. Ramesh Chand Goel

j) Length of the string is printed as the count of the number of **characters:**
'P' , 'r' , 'a', 'k', 'r', 'i' , 't', 'i', ' ' '!'.

10

k) The count() function of string library counts the occurrences of the given character in the given string. As 'e' occurs 4 times in given string "Amit is elder to Sandeep". The output is:

4

l) The find() function in string library finds the first occurrence of the character given as argument and returns its index. The first

10

m) The join() function of string library prints the first string with characters of second in beginning and end :

'T Bennett Colman and Co. Ltd. O Bennett Colman and Co. Ltd. I'

n) The arithmetic expression inside the string format is evaluated and the result is printed on the screen:

75.0

o) The string will be compared based on their ASCII values:

"Your word Banana , comes after Apple"

p) An invalid syntax error will be reported by Python IDLE because there is text written after the closing quote in first print().

For the second print(), the output will be a string where isn't will be printed as it is and ' will not be considered as a closing quote for print(). This is due to use of '\' to escape the next character as its regular meaning and print as it is on the screen.

"It isn't true" Vishal said.

q) The capitalize() function of string library converts the first character to capital and rest all characters in small letters.

Deepak is very loving and caring!

r) The lower() function of string library converts all characters in small letters.

gariyasi prakriti anrav ayushi ishaan

s) The split() function from string library separates the contents of the string as separate strings and return as a list:

['Krishna', 'Ajay', 'Monika']

t) The replace() function in string module replaces the given string with another one.

'I am proud to be Hindustani '

u) The split() function splits the given string into a list:

['Did', 'you', 'smile', 'today', '?']

v) The program removes every character at even place.
The output will be:

abcdefghi

w) The split() function splits the given string into a list of 2 strings. The string 'Peter' will be inserted at 2nd place in given list. The join() function again converts the list of 3 strings into a single string.

The output will be: **"John Peter Parera"**

x) The split('-') function creates a list by removing hyphens from the given string i.e. ['cock', 'bear', 'seal', 'cow']. The function sort() sorts the list alphabetically i.e. ['bear', 'cock', 'cow', 'seal']. The function join('-') again creates a list joined with hyphen '-'.

The output will be:**"bear-cock-cow-seal"**

y) The Python program given reads two integers representing a month and day and prints the season for that month and day.

For input: February and 20
The output is:

"Season is autumn"

z) The Python function given takes a string as input and add 'ing' at the end of it. It does not add 'ing' if the given string already ends with 'ing'.

The output will be:

flying

crying

string

7.2

i. True: str(47) will store integer 47 as '47'.

ii. True

   A positive index i+1 means i^{th} character from beginning of the string while a negative index –i means i^{th} character from end of the string.

iii. False

   It returns sub-string s[x] to s[y-1].

iv. False

   String slicing using s[:i] returns a sub-string from beginning to s[i-1].

v. True

vi. True

vii. False: A string in Python cannot be changed.

viii. False: Strings are not mutable in Python.

ix. True

   This is because it does not affect existing string 'word', but just returns a new string as 'Jtring'.

x. False

   It is a valid statement because it does not affect existing string 'w' but just returns a new string as 'Strdoc'.

Sets and Dictionaries

In this chapter you will be able to check how much you know about sets and dictionaries in Python.

Important term: Dictionaries are also known as Associative Memories or Associative Arrays.

Q.8.1 **What will be the output of the following commands?**

(a) >>> set_of_color = {'red', 'blue', 'green', 'red', 'orange'}
      >>> set_of_color

(b) >>> set_of_dishes = {'pasta', 'dosa', 'noodles'}
      >>> 'poha' in set_of_dishes

(c) >>> breakfast = set('Parantha')
      >>> breakfast

(d) >>> breakfast = set('Parantha')
      >>> dinner = set('Rice')
      >>> breakfast - dinner

(e) >>> breakfast = set('Parantha')
      >>> dinner = set('rice')
      >>> breakfast - dinner

(f) >>> a = set('Happiness')
      >>> b = set('Honesty')
      >>> a | b

(g) Consider the two sets a and b in 8.1(f), what will be the output of the following command?

      >>> a & b

(h) Consider the two sets a and b in 8.1(f), what will be the output of the following command?

>>> a ^ b

(i) >>>a = {x for x in 'mohanjadaro' if x not in 'mod'}

(j) >>> a = {1,2 , 3+4, 10*7}
>>> b = {7,14,21}
>>> a – b

(k) >>> num = {1:'One', 2: 'Two', 3: 'Three'}
>>> num

(l) >>> prizes = {'1st': 'Gold', '2nd' : 'Silver', '3rd': 'Bronze'}
>>> list(prizes)

(m) >>> levels = {1: 'Easy', 2 : 'Medium', 3: 'Hard'}
>>> list(levels. keys())

(n) >>>auth={'C':'Ritchie', 'Python':'Vassum','Pascal':'Pascal'}
>>> sorted(auth. keys())

(o) >>> a = {1:4, 2:7, 3:1}
>>> sorted(a.values())

(p) >>>dict([(1,'mon'),(2,'tues'),(3,'wed'),(4,'thu'),(5,'fri')])

(q) >>> dict(jan=1,feb=2)

(r) >>> months = {1:'jan', 2:'feb', 3:'mar', 4:'apr', 5:'may'}
>>> 'nov' in months

(s) >>> world = {1: 'war', 2: 'harmony', 3: 'peace'}
>>> del world[1]
>>>world

(t) >>> {x: x**3 for x in (10, 20, 30)}

Q.8.2 State whether the following statements are True or False:

i. {} can be used to create an empty set.

ii. All elements in a set are unordered.

iii. One set value can be assigned to another set value using = operator.

iv. The elements in a set cannot be changed.

v. del statement can be used to delete a set.

vi. Dictionaries are indexed by key which can be mutable.

vii. The keys in a dictionary should be unique.

viii. del statement can be used to delete a key:value pair in a dictionary.

ix. Lists can be used as a key in the dictionary.

x. The function list(d.keys( )) on a dictionary d returns a list of all the keys used in the dictionary in the sorted order of keys.

ANSWERS

8.1

a) The elements in a pair of curly braces indicate a set. The elements are unordered in a set. There are total six values initialized in the set 'set_of_color'. The duplicate elements are removed from a set automatically and the unordered output is:

{'red', 'blue', 'orange', 'green'}

b) The 'in' operator is used to test membership of an element in given set. It returns True if the element is a member of the set and returns False if the member is not a member of the set. Since element 'poha' is not a member of the set 'set_of_dishes', output is:

False

c) A set can also be created using set() function. The expected output is breakfast = {'P','a','r','a','n','t','h','a'}. Since it is a set, duplicate elements are removed automatically and elements are unordered. The value of breakfast is:

{'h','n', 't', 'a', 'r', 'P'}

d) The '-' operator returns the difference of the element as excluding the elements on the set on right hand side from the set of elements on its left hand side. Since there is nothing common in elements of 'breakfast' and 'dinner', the result is the elements of the set breakfast:

{'h','n', 't', 'a', 'r', 'P'}

e) The '-' operator returns the difference of the element as excluding the elements on the set on right hand side from the set of elements on its left hand side. Since there is only single element 'r' common in elements of 'breakfast' and 'dinner', the result is the elements of the set breakfast except 'r':

{'a', 'P', 't', 'h', 'n'}

f) The ' I ' operator is used to perform the union of the two sets. It returns the elements in two sets as its operands (set1 I set2) with duplicate elements removed.

{'n', 'y', 'p', 'a', 't', 'H', 'i', 'e', 's', 'o'}

g) The '&' operator is used to perform the intersection of the two sets. It returns the elements in two sets as its operands (set1 & set2) with elements common in both sets.

{'H', 'e', 's', 'n'}

h) The '^' operator is used to find the symmetric difference in the two sets. It returns the elements in two sets as its operands (set1 ^ set2) with elements in set1 and set2 but not in both sets.

{'a', 'i', 'p', 'y', 't', 'o'}

i) List comprehensions can also be used in a set. The value of set 'a' is the elements other than 'm', 'o' and 'd' in set {'m', 'o', 'h', 'a', 'o', 'n', 'j', 'o', 'd', 'a', 'r', 'o' }

{'j', 'a', 'h', 'r', 'n'}

j) The elements present in set 'a' are returned after removing the elements in the set 'b'. The arithmetic expressions are first evaluated and then compared.

{1, 2, 70}

k) {1: 'One', 2: 'Two', 3: 'Three'}

Important terms: By giving a key : value pairs separated by commas in a curly braces {}, 'num' is defined as a dictionary. Unlike a sequence, the values are indexed by corresponding keys.

l) list(d) function returns the list of all keys in unsorted order in the dictionary d .

['1st', '2nd', '3rd'] or ['1st', '3rd', '2nd']

m) list(d.keys()) function returns the list of all keys in unsorted order in the dictionary d.

[1,2,3] or [3,1,2]

n) The function sorted(d.keys()) returns the list of all keys in the dictionary d in the sorted order.

['C', 'Pascal', 'Python']

o) The function sorted(d.values()) returns the list of all values in the dictionary d in the sorted order.

[1, 4, 7]

p) The dict() construct is used to create an unnamed dictionary. The key value pairs are to be given in pair of parentheses separated by a comma.

{ 1: 'mon', 2: 'tues', 3: 'wed', 4: 'thu', 5: 'fri'}

q) This is easy way to create an unnamed dictionary of the keys are strings.

{'jan': 1, 'feb': 2}

r) The 'in' operator checks whether the value exists in the dictionary or not. It returns True if the value exists in the dictionary and False if it does not. Here, 'nov' is not present in any of the key value pairs in dictionary 'months'. The result is

False

s) del (d[key]) function deletes the key value pair with key value in dictionary d:

{2: 'harmony', 3: 'peace'}

t) The dictionary comprehensions are used and the keys are values of x as 10,20 and 30. The corresponding values are cube of the keys.

{10: 1000, 20: 8000, 30: 27000}

8.2

i. False
{} creates an empty dictionary. Only the function set( ) can be used to create an empty set.

ii. True

iii. True

iv. False
The elements in a set can be changed by assignment to a new value. For example, if there are two sets, a={1,2,3} and b= {2,3,4}, using a=a-b, a gets the value {1}.

v. True

vi. False

The keys which are used for indexing in dictionaries should be immutable. For example, strings and numbers can be the keys in a dictionary. Also the tuples with only immutable objects can be used as keys in a dictionary.

vii. True

viii. True

It can be done by specifying the name of the key whose value if to be deleted. del d[key] will delete the key:value pair from dictionary d.

ix. False

A list is a mutable data structure. It can be modified using many list manipulation methods and operations. So it cannot be used as a key value in a dictionary.

x. False

The function list(d.keys( )) returns the list of all the keys used in the dictionary in an arbitrary order. The function sorted(d.keys( )) should be used to get the elements in the dictionary in the sorted order.

Tuples

> *In this chapter you will be able to check how much you know about tuples in Python.*

Q.9.1 **What will be the value of 'data' after executing the following command(s)?**

(a) >>> data = 12,34,'Gariyasi', 'Prakriti', 19, 20

(b) Consider the tuple 'data' as defined in Q 9.1a, what will be the output of the following command?
>>>len(data)

(c) >>> t = 1,2,'3'
>>> x, y, z = t
>>>print(x, y, z,)

(d) >>> empty = ()
>>> print(empty)

(e) >>> one_value = 'hello'
>>> len(one_value)

(f) >>> one_value = 'hello',
>>> len(one_value)

(g) >>> single_tuple = 1,2,3,4
>>> nested_tuple =single_tuple , ('1st', '2nd', '3rd', '4th')

(h) >>> single_tuple = 1,2,3,4
>>> nested_tuple = single_tuple , ('1st', '2nd', '3rd', '4th')
>>> len(nested_tuple)

(i)   >>> tuple1 = 10, 'Ten', 100, 'Hundred'
       >>> x,y,z = tuple1

(j)   >>>u = 'We', 'are', 'proud', 'to', 'be', 'an', 'Indian'
       >>>u[0] = [1,2]

Q.9.2   **State whether the following statements are True or False:**

   i.   A tuple need not be parenthesized.

  ii.   A tuple is a sequence type data like lists.

 iii.   A tuple is mutable like a list.

 iv.   A tuple can contain mutable objects.

  v.   The elements of a tuple are heterogeneous while that of a list are homogenous.

ANSWERS

9.1

a) The variable 'data' is defined as tuple in Python. All the values separated by comma are packed together in the given sequence in tuple 'data'. The value of 'data' is:
(12, 34, 'Gariyasi', 'Prakriti', 19, 20)

b) The len() function returns the number of elements in the tuple:

6

c) When a tuple is packed with some values, it is called tuple packing. In case the values are to be unpacked to different variable given in a sequence, then it is called sequence unpacking. As tuple t has 3 values in a sequence, so the three variables x,y,z get the values 1,2,'3' respectively. The values of x, y and z will be printed on the same line on the screen because there is one trailing comma in print():

1, 2, '3'

d) An empty tuple contains as empty set of parentheses (). Output will be:

()

e) The variable one_value is assigned a string value 'hello'......... Thus it is considered as a string variable. The len() function returns the length of the characters in the string 'hello':

5

f) The variable one_value is assigned a string value 'hello' followed by a trailing comma(,). Thus it is considered as a tuple. The len() function returns the number of the characters in the tuple which is only the string 'hello':

1

g) Using a comma(,) operator causes nesting of two tuples. So the contents of nested_tuple are:
((1,2,3,4), ('1st', '2nd', '3rd', '4th'))

h) The len() function returns the number of elements in the tuple 'nested_ tuple'. As the elements are two tuples. So the output is: **2**

i) The sequence unpacking takes place here. The values on left side of the sequence should be the same as the values on right side. Single 'tuple1' is assigned 4 values while there are only 3 variables x,y and z, following error is reported by Python IDLE:

ValueError: too many values to unpack (expected 3)

j) A tuple is used to store a sequence of any type of datatypes. But the tuples are immutable i.e. we cannot change the values assigned to its elements. So following error is reported by Python IDLE:
TypeError: 'tuple' object does not support item assignment

9.2

i. False: Error will be shown if parentheses are missing.

ii. True

iii. False, a tuple is immutable

iv. True

v. False: It is not mandatory.

Chapter 10

Classes

> *In this chapter you will be able to check how much you know about classes in Python.*

Q.10.1 **What will be the output after executing the following programs in Python?**

(a)

```
class Human:
    def __init__(self, name, age):
        self.name = name
        self.age = age

    def display(self):
        print ("Name : ", name, ", Age: ", age)
e1 = Human("Sandeep", 30)
e1.display()
```

(b)

```
class Human:
    def __init__(self, name, age):
        self.name = name
        self.salary = age

    def display(self):
        print ("Name : ", self.name, ", Age: ", self.age)
e1 = Human("Ashu", 30)
e1.display()
```

(c)

```
class Person:
    def __init__(self, n, g):
        self.name = n
        self.gender = g
    def display(self):
        print ("Name : ", self.n, ", Gender : ", self.g)
e1 = Person("Shikha", "Female")
e1.display()
```

(d)

```
class KGStudent :
    def __init__(self, name, marks):
        self.name = name
        self.marks = marks

    def display():
        print ("Name : ", self.name, ", Marks: ", self.marks)
c1=KGStudent("Ishaan", 100)
c1.display()
```

(e)

```
class KGStudent:
    def __init__(self, name, marks):
        self.name = name
        self.marks = marks

    def display(self):
        print ("Name : ", self.name, ", Marks: ", self.marks)
c1=KGStudent("Arnav", 100)
c1.display()
```

(f)

```
class GovtEmployee:
    def __init__(self, name, salary):
        self.name = name
        self.salary = salary

    def displayEmp(self):
        print ("Name : ", self.name, ", Salary: ", self.salary)
```

```
elist=[]
for i in range(3):
    n=input("Enter name of an employee: ")
    s=int(input("Enter salary of an employee: "))
    e=GovtEmployee(n,s)
    elist.append(e)
for e in elist:
    e.displayEmp()
```

(g)

```
class PGStudent:
    def __init__(self, name, marks):
        self.name = name
        self.marks = marks

    def displayS(self):
        print ("Name : ", self.name, ", Marks: ", self.marks)
slist=[]
for i in range(3):
    n=input("Enter name of the student: ")
    m=int(input("Enter marks of the student: "))
    s=PGStudent(n,m)
    slist.append(s)
max=-1
s1= ""
for s in slist:
s.displayS()
if s.marks>max:
    max=s.marks
    s1=s.name
print("Student with max marks:", s1)
```

(h)

```
class Kid:
    kidsCount = 0

    def __init__(self, name, house):
```

```python
        self.name = name
        self.house = house
        Kid.kidsCount += 1
    def displayCount(self):
        print( "Total Kids: ", Kid.kidsCount)
    def displayKid(self):
        print ("Name : ", self.name, ", House: ", self.house)
k1=Kid("Ayushi", "Air")
k1.displayKid()
k1.displayCount()

n=input("Enter name of a kid: ")
h=int(input("Enter house of a kid: "))
k=Kids(n,h)
k.displayKid()
k.displayCount()
```

(i)

```python
class Point3D:
    counter=0
    def __init__(self, x, y,z):
        self.x = x
        self.y = y
        self.z = z
        Point3D.counter+=1

    def displayPoint3D(self):
        print("x= ",self.x, "y= ", self.y, "z=", self.z)
    def countPoints(self):
        print(Point3D.counter)
p1=Point3D(12,10,10)
p1.displayPoint3D()
p2=Point3D(2,10,20)
p2.displayPoint3D()
p1.countPoints()
p2.countPoints()
```

(j)

```
class Faculty:
    def __init__(self, firstname, lastname, age):
        self.firstname = firstname
        self.lastname = lastname
        self.age=age

    def displayInfo(self):
        print("Name: ", self.firstname + " " + self.lastname)
        print("Age: ", self.age)

class Teacher():
    def __init__(self, first, last, age, sttaffnum, subject):
        super().__init__(first, last,age))
        self.staffnumber = staffnum
        self.subject= subject

    def displayTeacher(self):
        super().displayInfo()
        print("Staff no.= ", self.staffnumber)
        print("Subject = ", self.subject)

x = Faculty ("Usha", "Goel", 24)
y = Teacher ("Ramesh", "Goel", 34, 101, "Mathematics")

x.displayInfo ()
y.displayTeacher ()
```

(k)

```
class Faculty:
    def __init__(self, firstname, lastname, age):
        self.firstname = firstname
        self.lastname = lastname
        self.age=age

    def displayInfo(self):
        print("Name: ", self.firstname, " ",self.lastname, ", Age: ",
self.age)

class Teacher(Faculty):
```

```
        def __init__(self, first, last, age, sttaffnum, subject):
            super().__init__(first, last,age)
            self.staffnumber = staffnum
            self.subject= subject
        def displayTeacher(self):
            super().displayInfo()
            print("Staff no.= ", self.staffnumber,", Subject = ", self.subject)
    x = Person("Ashish", "Vidyarthi", 24)
    y = Employee("Homi", "Bhabha", 34,"1007")

    x = Faculty ("Usha", "Goel", 24)
    y = Teacher ("Ramesh", "Goel", 34, 101, "Mathematics")
    x.displayInfo ()
    y.displayTeacher ()
```

(1)

```
    class Book:
        def get(self):
            self.title = input("Enter title: ")
            self.author = int(input("Enter author: "))
            self.price=float (input("Enter price: "))

        def displayBook(self):
            print("Title:", self.title,", Author: ", self.author)
            print("Price: ", self.price)

    class Novel(Book):
        def getInfo(self):
            super().get()
            self.genre = input("Enter genre: ")

        def displayNovel(self):
            super().displayBook()
            print("Genre= ", self.genre)
    x1 = Book()
    x1.get()
```

y1 = Novel()

y1.getInfo()

x1.displayBook()

y1.displayNovel()

Q.10.2 State whether the following statements are True or False:

    i. If the name of the methods are display(self) in both - the base class and derived class in inheritance, then this is called method overloading.

    ii. Method overloading is not supported in Python.

    iii. We can access a class variable with any method in the class.

    iv. self can be used as the name for any of the argument in a method inside a class.

    v. The convention lower_case_with_underscores is used for functions, methods and classes in Python.

    vi. All exceptions in Python should be derived from class 'Exception'.

    vii. When an __init__() method is defined inside a class, class instantiation automatically invokes it for the newly-created class instance.

    viii. Base classes may override methods of their derived classes.

    ix. "Private" instance variables exist in Python that cannot be accessed except from inside an object.

    x. Any data variable/member should be accessed using self except class variable.

ANSWERS

10.1

(a) **NameError: name 'name' is not defined** will be displayed. This is because name and age should be referred by self.name and self. age instead of name and age.

(b) **Name : Ashu , Age : 30**

(c) **AttributeError: 'Person' object has no attribute 'n'**. This is because the variables inside __init__ function are the actual data members while the ones which are passed to it are formal arguments. self.name and self.gender should be used instead of self.n and self.g.

(d) **TypeError: display() takes 0 positional arguments but 1 was given.** This is because keyword self is missing in definition of display() function.

(e) **Name: Arnav, Marks: 100**

(f) The program input values for 3 GovtEmployees and appends them in a list, elist. Then it displays the details about these in given format:

Name : Gautam , Salary: 100000

Name : Sunil , Salary: 200000

Name : Anil , Salary: 300000

(g) The program input values for 3 PGStudents and prints the name of the student with highest marks:

Name : Jayanti , Marks: 99

Name : Aradhana , Marks: 99

Name : Vineeta , Marks: 100

Student with max marks: Vineeta

(h) The program creates a class Kid to store name and house of a child. A class variable kidsCount is initialized to 0. It is used to display the count of number of Kid objects created in the program.

Name : Ayushi , House: Air

Total Kids: 1

Enter name of a kid: [Kriti]

Enter house of a kid: [Water]

Name : Kriti , House: Water

Total Kids: 2

(i) The program creates a class for representing 3D point objects and displays the total count using class variable counter. The value of counter is displayed as same by both the objects.

x= 12 y=10 z=10

x= 2 y= 10 z=20

2

2

(j) The program gives error because the base class from which Teacher class is derived is not defined while defining it.

TypeError: object.__init__() takes no parameters

(k) The program creates a class Faculty and derives a class Teacher from it. The methods of base class are called from derived class using the keyword super(). One object of type Faculty and one of type Teacher are created and details are displayed using their respective display methods:

Name: Usha Goel, Age: 24

Name: Ramesh Goel, Age: 34

Staff no.= 101, Subject = Mathematics

(l) The program creates a class Book and derives a class Novel from Book. The methods of base class are called from derived class using the keyword super(). One object of type Novel is created. There is no __init__() function here. So no value is passed while creating object of this class. The values are read from user using getInfo() method and details are displayed using displayNovel() method.

Enter title: The God of Small Things

Enter author: Arundhati Roy Enter price= 400

Enter genre: Literature fiction

Title: The God of Small Things, Author: Arundhati Roy

Price:400

Genre: Literature fiction

10.2

i. False

if the name of the methods are display(self) in both - the base class and derived class, then this is called method overriding.

ii. True

iii. True

iv. False

self should always use as the name for the first method argument

v. False

The convention is to use CamelCase for classes and lower_case_with_ underscores is used for functions and methods.

vi. True

vii. True

viii. False

Derived classes may override methods of their base classes.

ix. False

Such concept does not exist in Python.

x. True

Files

In this chapter you will be able to check how much you know about file handling in Python.

11.1 Consider using open function for opening a file:

> filename = input('Enter a filename : ')
>
> f1 = open(filename, 'mode')

Which of the following modes is used when a file is to be opened forwriting only?

    (a) w

    (b) w+

    (c) a

    (d) All of these

11.2 Consider using open function for opening a file:

> filename = input('Enter a filename : ')
>
> f1 = open(filename, 'mode')

Which of the following modes is used when a file is to be opened for both reading and writing?

    (a) rw

    (b) w+

    (c) r+

    (d) w

11.3 Consider using open function for opening a file:

> filename = input('Enter a filename : ')
>
> f1 = open(filename, 'mode')

Which of the following modes is used when a file is to be opened for writing to an existing file without overwriting the existing contents?

    (a) wr

    (b) w+

    (c) a

    (d) None of these

11.4 Consider using open function for opening a file:

```
filename1 = input('Enter a filename : ')
file1 = open(filename1, 'mode')
```

Which of the following modes is used when a file is to be opened for reading only?

    (a) r

    (b) w

    (c) a

    (d) None of these

11.5 **What happens when the file with specified filename in the function open() does not already exist in the system using the command: file1=open(filename, 'w')?**

    (a) file1 gets a NULL value

    (b) a new file is created with given filename

    (c) an error message is shown "file does not exist"

    (d) None of these

11.6 **What happens when the file with specified filename in the function open does not already exist in the system using the command: file1=open(filename, 'r')?**

    (a) an error message is shown "file does not exist"

    (b) file1 gets a NULL value

    (c) a new file is created with given filename

    (d) None of these

11.7 Consider the program given:

```
name1 = input('Enter a filename : ')
f1 = open(name1, "w")
t1="This is content of the file"
f1.write(t1)
x1=f1.read()
print(x1)
f1.close()
```

What happens when a file name1 is opened for the writing in "w" mode and a read operation is performed?

    (a)   read operation is successfully performed

    (b)   an error message : "io.UnsupportedOperation: not readable"

    (c)   read operation returns blank

    (d)   None of these

11.8 Consider the program given:

```
name1 = input('Enter a filename : ')
f1 = open(name1, "w+")
t1="This is content of the file"
f1.write(t1)
x1=f1.read()
print(x1)
f1.close()
```

What happens when a file name1 is opened for the writing in "w+" mode and a read operation is performed?

    (a)   read operation is successfully performed

    (b)   an error message : "io.UnsupportedOperation: not readable"

    (c)   read operation returns blank

    (d)   None of these

11.9 Consider the program given:

```
name1 = input('Enter a filename : ')
f1 = open(name1, "r+")
f1.write("Hello this is written in a file.")
x1=f1.read()
print(x1)
f1.close()
```

What happens when an already existing file is opened for the writing and reading in "r+" mode and a read operation is performed?

    (a)   read operation is successfully performed and "Hello this is written in a file." is printed on the screen

    (b)   an error message is shown "FileNotFoundError: No such file or directory: name1"

    (c)   blank is returned from read operation

    (d)   None of these

11.10 Consider the program given:

```
name1 = input('Enter a filename : ')
f1 = open(name1, "r+")
f1.write("Hello this is written in a file.")
x1=f1.read()
print(x1)
f1.close()
```

What happens when a file which does not already exist is opened for the writing and reading in "r+" mode and a read operation is performed?

    (a)   read operation is successfully performed and "Hello this is written in a file." is printed on the screen

    (b)   an error message :"FileNotFoundError: No such file or directory: name1"

    (c)   blank is returned from read operation

    (d)   None of these

11.11 **What happens when the following program code in Python is executed?**

```
name1 = input('Enter a filename : ')
f1 = open(name1, "w")
t1=int(input('Enter your age:'))
f1.write(t1)
f1.close()
```

    (a)   Value of t1 will be written in file as integer

    (b)   Value of t1 will be written in file as a string

    (c)   An error message :TypeError: write() argument must be str, not int

    (d)   None of these

11.12 Consider the following program in Python:

```
name1 = input('Enter a filename : ')
f1 = open(name1, "w+")
t1=int(input('Enter your age:'))
f1.write(t1)
```

```
r1=f1.read()
print(r1)
f1.close()
```

What happens when the following program code in Python is executed and given input is entered by the user?

Enter a filename: a.dat

Enter your age: 40

(a) File 'a.dat' will be opened for writing and reading and error will be reported if 'a.dat' does not already exists. 40 will be written in 'a.dat' and also printed on screen.

(b) File 'a.dat' will be opened for writing and reading and if 'a.dat' does not already exists, it will be created. 40 will be written in 'a.dat' and also printed on screen.

(c) File 'a.dat' will be opened for writing and reading and if 'a.dat' does not already exists, it will be created. 40 will be written in 'a.dat' but will not be printed on screen.

(d) None of these

11.13 Consider the following program in Python:

```
name1 = input('Enter a filename : ')
f1 = open(name1, "w+")
t1=int(input('Enter your age:'))
f1.write(t1)
r1=f1.read()
f1.seek(0)
print(r1)
f1.close()
```

What happens when the following program code in Python is executed and given input is entered by the user?

Enter a filename: a.dat

Enter your age: 40

(a) File 'a.dat' will be opened for writing and reading and error will be reported if 'a.dat' does not already exists. 40 will be written in 'a.dat' and also printed on screen.

(b) File 'a.dat' will be opened for writing and reading and if 'a.dat' does not already exists, it will be created. 40 will be written in 'a.dat' and also printed on screen.

(c) File 'a.dat' will be opened for writing and reading and if 'a.dat' does not already exists, it will be created. 40 will be written in 'a.dat' but will not be printed on screen.

(d) None of these

11.14 Consider that file 'myfile.dat' has the contents:

This is a new file where we are writing. There are seven days in a week. There are twelve months in a year.

What will be the output of the following program in Python?

```python
# readFile1.py

def readFile1(name):
    f1 = open(name, "r")
    while True:
        text = f1.read(50)
        if text == "":
            break
        print(text)
    f1.close()
readFile1('myfile.dat ')
```

(a) Entire text will be read in variable text and printing on screen

(b) 50 characters will be read in variable 'text' and printing on screen

(c) An error message will be shown as: wrong input to read()

(d) None of these

11.15 Consider the program given below:

```python
def copyFile(old, new):
    f1 = open( old, "r")
    f2 = open(new, "w")
    while True:
        text = f1.read()
        if text == "":
            break
        f2.write(text)
    f1.close()
    f2.close()
```

Assume that file 'source.dat' has the contents:

> This is a new file where we are writing.
>
> %There are seven days in a week.
>
> There are twelve months in a year.

What will be the output of the following command in Python?

>>> copyFile('source.dat', 'destination.dat')

(a)   contents of file 'source.dat' will be copied to 'destination.dat'.

(b)   contents of 'sourec.dat' will be printed on the screen

(c)   Error message will be shown that two files cannot be opened

(d)   None of these

11.16   What will be the output of the following commands?

(i)   >>> f = open('filename1', 'w')
      >>> f.read()

(ii)   >>> f = open('a.dat', 'w')
       >>> f.write('Welcome to first line of my file')

(iii)   >>> f = open('a.dat', 'w')
        >>> f.write('Welcome to first line of my file')
        >>>list(f)

(iv)   >>> f = open('a.dat', 'r')
       >>> f.close()
       >>> f.read()

(v)   >>>f = open('a.dat', 'w+')
      >>> f.write('Welcome to first line of my file. ')
      >>> f.write('Here comes the second line of my file. ')
      >>>f.write('Third line. ')
      >>>f.seek(0)
      >>> t=f.readlines()
      >>>print(t)

ANSWERS

11.1 a

11.2 b and c

Important terms: Mode "w+" means writing and reading and mode "r+" means reading and writing. File should be already existing when it is opened in "r+" mode while it will be created in "w+" mode if not existing already.

11.3 c

11.4 a

11.5 b

Since a file is opened for writing, a new file is created with given filename if it not already exists.

11.6 a

(an error message is shown "file does not exist")

11.7 b

(an error message is shown "io.UnsupportedOperation: not readable"

Here, the file is opened in "w" mode which means only writing. So system gives an error message when read operation is asked.

11.8 c

(blank is returned from read operation)

Here, read operation is performed successfully because the file is opened in "w+" mode which means writing and reading both. When the contents of t1 are written to the file, the position is at the end of the file. Hence, when read operation is performed, it reads end of file and returns blank.

11.9 c

(blank is returned from read operation)

Here, read operation is performed successfully because the already existing file is opened in "r+" mode which means writing and reading both. When the contents of t1 are written to the file, the position is at the end of the file. Hence, when read operation is performed, it reads end of file and returns blank.

11.10 b

(an error message is shown "FileNotFoundError: No such file or directory: name1")

Here, the file is opened in "r+" mode which requires a file to exist already. So a FileNotFoundError will be printed on the screen.

11.11 c

Here the contents are stored as string in files. So the integer value needs to be converted to a string using str(t1) before storing to the file.

11.12 c

File 'a.dat' will be opened for writing and reading and if 'a.dat' does not already exists, it will be created. 40 will be written in 'a.dat' but will not be printed on screen. This is because after writing the file object location is at the end of the file.

11.13 b

File 'a.dat' will be opened for writing and reading and if 'a.dat' does not already exists, it will be created. 40 will be written in 'a.dat' and also printed on the screen. This is because after writing f1.seek(0), the file object location is at the beginning of the file.

11.14 b

The contents of the file 'myfile.dat' will read 50 characters at a time and printed on the screen in three lines.

This is a new file where we are writing. There are

seven days in a week. There are twelve months in

a year.

11.15 a

The program copies the contents of file 'source.dat' to 'destination. dat'.

11.16

i. Whenever a text file 'filename' is opened using open, it can be opened it many modes: 'r' for only reading, 'w' for only writing, 'a' for appending to existing file and creating if a file is not already existing, 'r+' for reading and writing and 'r' is the default mode. Since file is opened here for writing mode, read() function is not permitted and following error message is shown.

io.UnsupportedOperation: not readable

ii. File with name 'a.dat' is created and opened in writing mode as it does not exist before. One line is written to it using f.write(). This function returns the total number of characters written in this file:

32

iii. The list(f) function reads and prints all the contents of the file. Since file is opened here for writing mode, list(f) function is not permitted and following error message is shown.

io.UnsupportedOperation: not readable

Important terms: The file should be closed using f.close() for writing and opened again for reading to use list(f) function.

iv. The file 'a.dat' is opened for reading. The function f.read() is called when it is closed. So no read can take place and the following error is reported:

ValueError: I/O operation on closed file

v. Three lines are written to file 'a.dat' using f.write() as it is opened for both writing and reading using 'w+' mode. f.readlines() will read all the lines in the file 'a.dat'.

['Welcome to first line of my file. Here comes the second line of my file. Third line']

Graphics

In this chapter you will be able to check how much you know about graphics in Python.

Q Select the most appropriate answer for the following questions:

12.1 Which of the following is used to create a top level window?

a) title()

b) Tk()

c) main()

d) All of these

12.2 Which of the following is used to set the window title?

a) title()

b) Tk()

c) geometry()

d) None of these

12.3 Which of the following is used to create a window icon?

a) geometry()

b) root()

c) wm_iconbitmap()

d) None of these

12.4 Which of the following is used to set window size?

a) geometry()

b) root()

c) wm_iconbitmap()

d) None of these

12.5 **Which of the following is used to display window and wait for any events?**

   a) root()
   b) wait()
   c) mainloop()
   d) None of these

12.6 **Which of the following is the datatype of a font in tkinter?**

   a) a list
   b) an integer
   c) a tuple
   d) None of these

12.7 **Which of the following represents red color?**

   a) #000000
   b) #0000ff
   c) #ff0000
   d) None of these

12.8 **Which of the following represents the shape of a canvas?**

   a) rectangular
   b) oval
   c) circle
   d) None of these

12.9 **Which of the following is used to add the canvas to the root window?**

   a) pack()
   b) add()
   c) join()
   d) Any of these

12.10 **Which of the following is used to create an arc in a window?**

   a) arc()
   b) createArc()
   c) create_Arc()
   d) create_arc()

12.11 **Which of the following is used to display an image in the canvas?**

   a) draw_image()
   b) create_image()

c) display_image()

d) None of these

12.12 **Which of the following represents the direction of the image in a canvas?**

a) anchor

b) dir

c) source

d) None of these

12.13 **Which of the following is a widget?**

a) Button

b) Label

c) Scrollbar

d) All of these

12.14 **Which of the following is an event handler?**

a) action()

b) bind()

c) pack()

d) None of these

12.15 **Which of the following is not a layout manager for arranging the widgets in a frame?**

a) pack layout manager

b) grid layout manager

c) place layout manager

d) None of these

12.16 **Which of the following is used to add a scrollbar to the Text widget?**

a) scrollbar()

b) ScrollBar()

c) Scrollbar()

d) None of these

12.17 **Which of the following is used to set the orientation of the scrollbar in a Text widget?**

a) orientation

b) Orientation

c) orient

d) None of these

12.18 **Which of the following widget allows the user to select values from a given set of values?**

a) Entry

b) Spinbox

c) Radiobutton

d) None of these

12.19 **Which of the following is not an option in "selectmode" in Listbox widget?**

a) browse

b) single

c) multiple

d) None of these

12.20 **Which of the following is used to add menu items to a menu?**

a) add_command()

b) add_value()

c) add_item()

d) None of these

12.21 **State whether the following statements are True or False:**

i.   Tk is a class whose object is to be created for creating a root window.

ii. A font represents a type of displaying only letters in a window.

iii. A frame is a container that is used to draw shapes like lines and curves.

iv. A canvas is a container that is used to display widgets like buttons and menus.

v.   pack() method is used to add a canvas to the root window.

vi. create_message() is used to display some text in the canvas.

vii. Checkbutton widget is used to allow the user to select one or more options from available group of options.

viii. Radiobutton widget allows the user to select only one option from a group of available options.

ix. Entry widget is used to create a rectangular box to enter or display one line of text.

x.   The bind() method is used to bind an event with an event handler function.

ANSWERS

12.1 b

12.2 a

12.3 c

12.4 a

12.5 c

12.6 c

12.7 c

12.8 a

12.9 a

12.10 d

12.11 b

12.12 a

12.13 d

12.14 b

12.15 d

12.16 c

12.17 c

12.18 b

12.19 d

12.20 a

12.21
    i. True

    ii. False

        It represents a type of displaying letters and numbers.

    iii. False

        A frame is a container that is used to display widgets like buttons and menus.

    iv. True

    v. True

    vi. False

        create_text() is used to display some text in the canvas.

    vii. True

    viii. True

    ix. True

    x. True

Built-in Functions

In this chapter you will be able to check how much you know about built-in functions in Python.

Q **Select the most appropriate answer for the following questions:**

13.1 Which of the following function returns the absolute value of a number, long integer or a floating point number?

   a) ord()

   b) chr()

   c) abs()

   d) None of these

13.2 Which of the following function returns True if any element of iterable is True?

   a) all()

   b) any()

   c) iter()

   d) None of these

13.3 Which of the following function takes an integer as argument and returns a character whose ASCII code is that integer?

   a) ord()

   b) chr()

   c) bin()

   d) None of these

13.4 **Which of the following function takes one character as input and returns the Unicode code as integer?**

   a) ord()
   b) chr()
   c) bin()
   d) None of these

13.5 **Which of the following function converts an integer into an octal string?**

   a) ord()
   b) oct()
   c) bin()
   d) None of these

13.6 **Which of the following function takes an object as input and returns a string containing a printable representation of an object?**

   a) repr()
   b) print()
   c) reload()
   d) None of these

13.7 **Which of the following function returns a new sorted list from the items in the iterable passed as argument?**

   a) list()
   b) sorted()
   c) slice()
   d) None of these

13.8 **Which of the following function returns a floating-point value number rounded to some digits after the decimal point?**

   a) round()
   b) setattr()
   c) slice()
   d) None of these

13.9 **Which of the following function retrieves the next item from the iterator?**

   a) next()
   b) range()
   c) slice()
   d) None of these

13.10 Which of the following function returns the smallest item in the given iterable or arguments(>=2)?

    a) min()
    b) hash()
    c) id()
    d) None of these

13.11 Which of the following function returns a floating-point number constructed from a number or a string?

    a) eval()
    b) float()
    c) bin()
    d) None of these

13.12 Which of the following function executes expressions or arbitrary code objects?

    a) eval()
    b) float()
    c) int()
    d) None of these

13.13 Which of the following function constructs a list from those elements of an iterable for which the function returns True?

    a) sorted()
    b) eval()
    c) filter()
    d) None of these

13.14 Which of the following function returns an enumerate object?

    a) iter()
    b) enumerate()
    c) filter()
    d) None of these

13.15 Which of the following function converts an integer number to a binary string?

    a) bin()
    b) oct()
    c) str()
    d) None of these

13.16 Which of the following function which returns a True or FALSE value of an expression?

   a) int()

   b) bool()

   c) hex()

   d) None of these

13.17 Which of the following function returns a complex number?

   a) getattr()

   b) complex()

   c) setattr()

   d) None of these

13.18 Which of the following is the return type of function globals() which returns the current global symbol table?

   a) A list

   b) A dictionary

   c) A tuple

   d) None of these

13.19 Which of the following function returns the hash value of an object?

   a) hash()

   b) id()

   c) ord()

   d) None of these

13.20 Which of the following function returns the identity of an object?

   a) hash()

   b) id()

   c) ord()

   d) None of these

13.21 What will be the output of the following commands?

   (i) >>> abs(-24.75)

   (ii) >>>any(x > 0 for x in [1,2,-3,-4])

(iii) >>>any(x > 0 for x in [-1,-2,-3,-4])

(iv) >>>all(x > 0 for x in [1,2,-3,-4])

(v) >>> x=10
      >>> eval('x +1')

(vi) >>> globals()

(vii) >>> locals()

(viii) >>> max([2,3,56,0,-9])

(ix) >>> hex(147)

(x) >>> bin(89)

ANSWERS

13.1 c
13.2 b
13.3 b
13.4 a
13.5 b
13.6 a
13.7 b
13.8 a
13.9 a
13.10 a
13.11 b
13.12 a
13.13 c
13.14 b
13.15 a
13.16 b
13.17 b
13.18 b
13.19 a
13.20 b

13.21

    i. 24.75

       abs() returns the absolute value.

   ii. True

       any() returns True if any element of the iterable is True.

  iii. False

       any() returns True if any element of the iterable is True. Since none of these is True, so the output is False.

  iv. False

       all() returns True if all elements of the iterable are True.

   v. 11

  vi. globals() returns a dictionary representing the current global symbol table

       {'__name__':'__main__','__package__': None, '__builtins__': <module 'builtins' (built-in)>, '__spec__': None, '__loader__': <class '_frozen_importlib.BuiltinImporter'>, '__doc__': None}

 vii. locals() returns a dictionary representing the current global symbol table

       {'__name__': '__main__', '__package__': None, '__builtins__': <module 'builtins' (built-in)>, '__spec__': None, '__loader__': <class '_frozen_importlib.BuiltinImporter'>, '__doc__': None}

 viii. 56

       max() returns the maximum value in the list.

  ix. '0x93'

       The hexadecimal equivalent of 147.

   x. '0b1011001'

       The binary equivalent of 89.

Miscellaneous

14.1 **What will be the output of the following command?**

>>> y = x +10

14.2 **What will be the output of the following commands?**

>>> x = '14'
>>> y = x+10

14.3 **What will be the output of the following command?**

>>> (5/(6-5+1))

14.4 **What will be the output of the following commands?**

>>> import math
>>> print(math.pi)

14.5 **What will be the output of the following commands?**

>>> f1 = 20.5
>>> product = f1 * s1

14.6 **What will be the output of the following commands?**

>>> import math
>>> random.random()

14.7 **What will be the output of the following commands?**

>>> import math
>>> data = [12.5, 71.75, 13.25, 10.75]
>>> statistics.mean(data)

14.8 **What will be the output of the following commands?**

>>> import math
>>> math.log(1000,2)

14.9 **What will be the output of the following command?**

>>> # print('Hurray! You are a master in Python! ')

14.10 **What will be the output of the following commands?**

```
>>> a=10
>>> b=20
>>> a,b = b,a
```

14.11 **What will be the output of the following command?**

```
>>>def table(n):
        i = 1
        while i <= 10:
            print(n,' * ', i, ' = ', n*i)
>>> table(3)
```

14.12 **What will be the output of the following command?**

```
>>> 'Hi Deepak! ' "How are you ? "
```

14.13 **What will be the output of the following command?**

```
>>> print(' C:\What is your \name' )
>>> print(r' C:\What is your \name' )
```

14.14 **What is the significance of the following command?**

```
>>>class MyError(Exception):
        def __init__(self, value):
            self.value = value
        def __str__(self):
            return repr(self.value)

    ....
```

14.15 **What will be the output of the following command?**

```
>>>chr(68)
```

14.16 **What will be the output of the following commands?**

```
>>> import sys
>>> print(sys.version)
```

14.17 **What will be the output of the following commands?**

```
>>> import sys
>>> print(sys.version_info)
```

14.18 **What will be the output of the following commands?**

```
>>> import os
>>> print(os.getcwd())
```

14.19 What will be the output of the following commands?

>>> import os
>>> print(os.getpid())

14.20 What is the significance of the following command?

>>> class A():

    pass

ANSWERS

14.1 **NameError: name 'x' is not defined**

Important term: A variable should be assigned a value before it can be used in an arithmetic expression.

14.2 The '+'operator can be used for arithmetic addition or for string concatenation. Here, one of the argument of binary operator '+' is a string and the other one is an integer. As first argument is a string, it is required to perform string concatenation. But, in the absence of a string as second argument, an error is reported:

TypeError: Can't convert 'int' object to str implicitly

14.3 The expression evaluates from left to right and the denominator turns out to be zero (6-(5+1)). So it becomes divide by zero which is reported as an exception in Python:

ZeroDivisionError: division by zero

14.4 By default, the pi value is stored as a double value

3.141592653589793

14.5 The '*' operator can be used for arithmetic multiplication or for string repetition. Here, one of the argument of binary operator '*' is a floating-point variable and the other one is a string. As first argument is a floating-point value, it is required to perform arithmetic multiplication. But, in the absence of a floating-point value or integer value as second argument, an error is reported:

TypeError: can't multiply sequence by non-int of type 'float'

14.6 The random() function is defined in random module. It is not a part of math library. So, following error will be reported because 'import random' is missing:

NameError: name 'random' is not defined

The output with import random is 0.43704553941814095

14.7 The statistics.mean() function is defined in statistics module. It is not a part of math library. So, following error will be reported because 'import statistics' is missing:

NameError: name statistics is not defined

The output with **import statistics** is 27.0625

14.8 The logarithm of 1000 base 2 will be printed:

9.965784284662087

14.9 Well, if you think it is : 'Hurray! You are a master in Python! '

Then it is wrong. This is because # in the beginning of the print() statement indicates to the Python interpreter that it is a single- line comment and it is not be interpreted for execution.

Important terms: The purpose of a comment is for documentation i.e. for writing information about the program, command, author, version or many such things which can help the developers as well as readers to understand in a better way. For example, # This is class that can help in database handling In case a number of lines or an entire sections of a Python code need not be executed but not deleted, it can be commented using three opening """ and three closing """.

14.10 The values of variables a and b will be swapped. This is a good use of tuples.

a = 20

b = 10

14.11 The output will be printing the following infinitely:

3* 1 = 3

This is due to the fact that the value of variable i has not been incremented in each iteration of the while loop and hence the condition i<10 is always True.

14.12 If you think it will give an error for not putting a '+' operator between two strings or error due to two types of quote ('Hi Deepak! ') and "How are you?" , then it is wrong. The strings written on command prompt one after the other are automatically concatenated irrespective of types of quotes used in each. The output is:

'Hi Deepak! How are you ?'

14.13 For the first print(), '\n' becomes the escape sequence and it is reserved for a newline. So the output is newline after your and rest of the characters of word name i.e. ame are printed on next line:

C:\What is your name

For the second print(), the output will be the printing of the entire string as such on the screen due to r character in the beginning. This asks the interpreter to take all strings as raw strings not considering any escape sequences. The output is:

C:\What is your \name

14.14 The argument in class definition indicates that MyException class has been derived from class Exception.

14.15 The character equivalent of ASCII code 68 will be printed on the screen: 'D'

14.16 print(sys.version) prints the current version of Python.

3.5.2 (v3.5.2:4def2a2901a5, Jun 25 2016, 22:01:18) [MSC v.1900 32 bit (Intel)]

14.17 print(sys.version_info) prints the details about the version of Python:

sys.version_info(major=3, minor=5, micro=2, releaselevel='final', serial=0)

14.18 The os module contains many functions. print(os.getcwd()) will print the current working directory on screen.

14.19 print(os.getpid()) function is in **os** module. It prints the process ID of the current process.

5884

14.20 It is used to create an empty class for future use.

Appendix A: Python keywords and their use

Table 1

Keyword	Meaning with example
and	It is a binary logical operator which returns False if any one of the operand is False and returns the value of the last operand if all its operands are True. >>> 47 and 56 >>>56
as	It is used to create a user defined name called alias while importing a module. >>> import math as m >>>print(m.cos(0)) 1.0
assert	It is used to debug the internal state of some assumptions. It is followed by a condition. Nothing happens if the condition is True but AssertionError is raised if the condition is False. >>> x=10 >>>assert x>=10 >>>assert x<10 Traceback (most recent call last): File "string", line 1, in <module> assert x<10 AssertionError An error message can also be passed with assert to be printed with Assertionerror. >>>assert x<10, "x is not less than 10" Traceback (most recent call last): File "string", line 1, in <module> assert x<10 AssertionError: x is not less than 10

break	It is a statement which ends the current loop and takes the control out of the current loop.
	for i in range(10):
	    if i%3==0:
	        break
	    else:
	        print(i)
	The loop is to vary from 0 to 9. But 3 is divisible by 3 and hence break causes the loop to exit. So only 0 1 2 are printed.

class	It is used to create a class with related data members and methods to operate on that data.
	class C1:
	    def __init__():
	      .....
	    def _method1():
	      ....

continue	It is used to control the flow in a loop. Wherever continue appears, the current iteration of the loop is ended and loop continues to next iteration.
	for i in range(10):
	    if i%3==0:
	        continue
	    else:
	        print(i)
	The loop is to vary from 0 to 9. But 3, 6 and 9 are divisible by 3 and hence continue skips printing 3, 6 and 9. So only 0 1 2 4 5 7 8 are printed.

def	It is used to define a user-defined function.
	    def sum(a,b):
	        print(a**2+b**2)

del	Everything is an object in Python. del is used to delete the reference to an object.
	>>>x=10
	>>>del x
	>>>x
	Traceback (most recent call last):
	    File "<string>", line 1, in <module>
	      x
	NameError: name 'x' is not defined

if
else
elif
	These are used in if-elif-else ladder.
	a1= 10
	if a>0:
	    print("a is positive")
	elif a==0:
	    print("a is zero")
	else:
	    print("a is negative")
	Output will be "a is positive"

except
raise
try
finally
	These are used in handling exceptions in Python. The statements which can cause exceptions or errors are placed inside a try.. except block. The exception is raised using raise.
	
	try:
	    a = int(input())
	    b= a-5
	    c=a/b
	    raise ZeroDivisionError("cannot divide")
	    raise ValueError("Wrong input")
	
	except ZeroDivisionError:
	    raise
	except ValueError:
	    raise
	finally:
	    print(c)
	When value of a is input as 5:
	Traceback (most recent call last):
	    File "<string>", line 1, in <module>
	        c=a/b
	ZeroDivisionError: cannot divide
	
	When value of a is input as a string:
	Traceback (most recent call last):
	    File "<string>", line 1, in <module>
	        A=int(input())
	ValueError: wrong input
	Otherwise value of c is printed.

False	It is a truth value in Python. A boolean(or logical) operation or comparison operation may result in a False value. It means 0. >>> 5>7 False
for	It is a statement which allows us to repeat a set of statements together for a number of times. for i in range(1,6,2): print(i) The loop variable i varies from 1 to 5 (6 not included) and is incremented by 2. It prints 1,3 and 5.

global	It is used to declare that a variable inside the function is global i.e. outside the local scope of function.
	
	``python
	g_var = 20
	def fun_read():
	    print(g_var)
	def fun_write():
	    global g_var
	    g_var =200
	fun_read()
	fun_write()
	fun_read()
	``
	
	The output will be:
	20
	200

from import	import is used to import all attributes of modules into the current namespace.
	>>>import math
	We need to use name of module with evry attribute for using:
	>>>print(math.pi)
	
	If we want to import only specific attribute from the module, we can use from..import
	>>> from math import pi
	
	Then we can directly write only the name of the attribute
	>>> print(pi)

in	It is sued to test if a value is contained in a sequence (list, tuple, string etc.). It returns True if the value is present and False if it is not. >>> 6 in [1,3] False

is	It is used in Python to test identity of an object. It returns True if two variables are referring to the same object.
	>>> 5 is 6
	False
	>>> True is True
	True

lambda	It is used to create a function with no name and return statement. It contains only only expression for evaluation:
	>>> a = lambda a1: a1*2
	>>> for i in range(1,3):
	    print(a(i))
	It will print
	1
	4
	6

None	It is a special constant in Python. It represents that the value is either null or is missing. It is not False i.e. 0 or an empty list, dictionary, string etc. A function returns None if there is no return statement in it. We can assign a particular variable a value None: x=None

nonlocal	It is used to declare a variable inside a nested function which is not local to it.
	
	def fun_outer():
	    x= 10
	    def fun_inner():
	        nonlocal x
	        x =20
	        print("Inner function value of x: ", x)
	    fun_inner()
	    print("Outer function value of x: ", x)
	fun_outer()
	
	The output will be:
	Inner function value of x: 20
	Outer function value of x: 20

not	It is a unary logical operator which returns False if the operand is True and returns True if the operand is False. >>> not(47 or 56) False
or	It is a binary logical operator which returns False if all of the operands are False and returns the value of the first True operand and does not evaluates rest. >>> 47 or 56 47

pass	It is a null statement in Python. It is just a placeholder. It is used in creating empty function or class:
	def f1():
	    pass
	class C:
	    pass

return	It is used inside a function. The function returns the value and exits when there is a return statement.
	def f(a,b):
	    c = a+b
	    if c>100:
	        return c
	    c = a-b
	    print(c)
	>>> f(34,90) will return after printing 124.

True	It is a truth value in Python. A boolean(or logical) operation or comparison operation may result in a True value. It means 1.
	>>> 5<7
	>>> True

while	It is a statement which allows us to repeat a set of statements together for a number of times.
	i=1
	while a<6:
	    print(i)
	    i=i+2
	The loop variable i varies from 1 to 5 (6 not included) and is incremented by 2. It prints 1,3 and 5.

with	It is used to wrap the execution of a block of code within methods defined by the context manager. In a nested block, one needs to execute the methods __exit__ and __enter__. These are implemented in class called context manager. with open("a.txt", 'w') as file1: file1.write('Writing in the file') It automatically closes the file after the nested block of code.

yield	It is used inside a function like a return statement and it returns a generator which generates one item at a time. Thus it saves a lot of memory.
	def gen():
	    for i in range(3):
	        yield i*i
	g=gen()
	for a in g:
	    print(a)
	This will print
	0
	1
	4

Appendix B: Operators in Python and their precedence

Table 2

Operator	Description	No. of operands	Example
**	Exponentiation (raise to the power)	2	$2**3=2^3=8$
~ + -	Complement Unary plus Unary minus	1 1 1	~(42) = False +45 -67
* / % //	Multiply Divide Modulo Floor division	2 2 2 2	5*4=20 40/6=6.66 40%3= 1 40//6=6
+ -	Binary addition Binary subtraction	2 2	78+10=88 78-10=68
>> <<	Bitwise Right shift Bitwise Left shift	2 2	4>>1 = 2 4<<1= 8
&	Bitwise 'AND'	2	4&1 = 0
^ |	Bitwise exclusive 'OR' Logical 'OR'	2 2	4^1 = 5 4|1 = 5
 <= < > >=	Comparison operators Less than or equal to Less than More than More than or equal to	 2 2 2 2	 5<=8 = True 8 <7 = False 7 >8 = False 9>=8 = True
 = = !=	Equality operators Equal to Not equal to	 2 2	 6==6 True 6!=7 False
 = %= *= **= /= //= -= +=	Assignment operators Assignment	 2 2 2 2 2 2 2 2	 x=5 →x=5 x%=2 →x=1 x*=3 → x= 3 x**=3 → x=27 x/=2 → x=13.5 x//=3 → x=4 x-=1 → x=3 x+=2 → x=5

is is not	Identity operators	2 2	x,y=2,3 x is y→False x,y=2,3 x is not y→True
in not in	Membership operators	2 2	'h' in 'Hello' True 1 not in [1,2] False
not or and	Logical operators	1 2 2	not(3&4)=True 3 or 4 = 3 3 and 4 = 4

Appendix C: Libraries in Python & common functions

Table 3

Library	Common functions
BeautifulSoup	It provides functions for xml and html parsing
IPython	It is a python prompt on steroids
matplotlib	It is a numerical plotting library
nltk	It helps in string manipulation (Natural Language Toolkit)
Nose	It is a testing framework for Python
NumPy	It provides advances mathematical functions
Pillow	It provides functions for handling images
Pygame	It provides functions for 2 dimensional programs for games
Pyglet	It is a 3 dimensional animation and gaming creation engine
pyGtk	It is a GUI toolkit
pyQT	It is a GUI toolkit
pywin32	It provides some useful methods and classes for interacting with windows
Requests	It is library which provides functions for http
Scapy	It is a packet sniffer and analyser for python
SciPy	It is a library of algorithms and mathematical tools
Scrapy	It provides functions for webscraping
SQLAlchemy	It is a database library
SymPy	It provides functions for algebraic evaluation, differentiation, expansion, complex numbers, etc.
Twisted	It deals with network application development
wxPython	It is a GUI toolkit

Bibliography

Following books/websites have been referred for learning Python along with Python documentation:

www.python.org

www.learnpython.org

www.tutorialpoints.com/python

www.w3resource.com/python

Learning with Python by Jeffrey Elkner, Dreamtech publications

Core Python Programming by R Nageswara Rao, Dreamtech publications

Computation and Programming Using Python, by John V. Guttag, Prentice Hall of India

MODEL TEST PAPER 1

Attempt all questions

Maximum Marks 100   **Time allowed : 3 Hrs**

Q.1(a) Explain various forms of 'for' loop in Python with suitable examples.
(5)

Q.1(b) Explain various operations which can be performed on a dictionary in Python. (5)

Q.2 (a) Explain various bitwise operators in Python. Explain the functioning of each with suitable examples   . (5)

Q.2 (b) Explain differences between list and a tuple in Python.   (5)

Q.3 Write and explain the output of the following commands in Python: (4×5=20)

(a) >>>20+5 | 2>>2**2%3

(b) n=0
q= "What is the result of 2*10, 4*5?"
while n!= "20":
        n=input(q)
print("Correct answer":)

(c) >>>list1= [4,2,3,4,5,4,6,7]
>>>print(list1.count(4))

(d) >>>n= ["Aamir" , " Salman" , " Shahrukh"]
>>>print(n[-1][-2])

Q.4 Find out errors in the following programs in Python: (4×5=20)

(a) >>> n = [1, 2, 3, 0, Red]

(b) enum = []
for n in l:
if n % 2 == 0
        enum.append(n)
return enum

(c) >>> n = [1, 2, 3, 4]
>>> for i in range(1,5):
        print(i)

(d) >>>print(hello how are you?)

Q.5 (4×10=40)

(a) Write a program in Python to divide the contents of a list into two lists with even and odd numbers separately.

(b) Write a program in Python which inputs distance in feet and prints it in inches, yards and miles.

(c) Write a program in Python to find sum of series: $x^1 + x^2 + \ldots + x^n$.

(d) A prime number is an integer greater than 1 that is divisible only by 1 and itself. For example, 2 and 7 are prime numbers. Write a program in Python which inputs a number from user and then displays a message indicating whether the number is prime or not.

Answers Model Test Paper 1:

1(a) There are many forms in which we can use for loop. First form is: **for variable1 in range(*terminating_value*):**

Here the initial value of loop variable variable1 is zero(0) by default and the loop variable changes value from 0 upto *terminating_value* (not including *terminating_value*). The value of loop variable is incremented by 1.

For example, to find the sum of the series: 0+1+2+3 for loop will be:

```
sum=0
for i in range(4):
    sum+=i
print(sum)
```

The second form is:

for variable1 in range(*initial_value, terminating_value*):

Here the initial value of loop variable variable1 can be specified by the user and the loop variable changes value from *initial_value* upto *terminating_value* (not including *terminating_value*). The value of loop variable is incremented by 1.

For example, to print the numbers from 101 to 105, for loop will be:

```
for i in range(101,106):
    print(i)
```

Third form is:

for variable1 in range(*initial_value, terminating_value, update_value*):

Here the initial value of loop variable variable1 can be specified by the user and the loop variable changes value from *initial_value* upto *terminating_value* (not including *terminating_value*). The value of loop variable is updated by given *update_value*.

For example, to find the sum: 2+4+6+8+10, for loop will be: loop will be:

```
sum=0
for i in range(2,11,2):
    sum+=i
print(sum)
```

Fourth form is:

for variable1 in list:

This is for accessing each value in the list one by one.

For example, to find the sum of all elements in a given list, for loop will be:

```
sum=0
list1= [11,20,13,47]
for element in list1:
    sum+=element
print(sum)
```

(b) In a dictionary, many {key:value} pairs are stored.

For example

>>> dict= {'First':1, 'Second':2, 'Third':3}

This means in dictionary dict, value is 1 for key 'First', value is 2 for key 'Second' and value is 3 for key 'Third'.

The main operations on a dictionary are storing a value with some key and extracting the value given the key.

>>>dict['First']

1

We can also change the value associated with a key:

>>> dict['First']= 13

>>>dict['First']

13

We can print all keys of a dictionary in a list using list(dict.keys())

>>>list(dict(keys())

["First", "Second", "Third"]

We can sort the keys using sorted(dict.keys())

>>>sorted(dict.keys())

['First', 'Second', 'Third']

We can also check whether the value is present in the dictionary:

>>>"First" in dict

True

A key-value pair can be deleted using del dict[key]

>>>del dict['Second']

>>>dict

{'First':1, 'Third':3}

2(a)   Various bitwise operators in Python are:

& : It returns bitwise ANDing of two numbers: 3&4 means 011 & 100, gives 000 i.e.0

| : It returns bitwise ORing of two numbers: 3|4 means 011 | 100, gives 111 i.e. 7

^: It returns bitwise XORing of two numbers 3^4 means 011 ^ 100, gives 111 i.e. 7

>>: It shifts the number right by n bits. 4>>1 gives 010 i.e. 2.

<<: It shifts the number left by n bits. 4<<1 gives 1000 i.e. 8

2(b)   In a list the elements are separated by comma and enclosed in square brackets while in a tuple, the elements are not enclosed in square brackets but separated by comma. A list is mutable, i.e. we can change the contents of a list while the contents of a tuple cannot be changed.

3(a)   25

3(b)   The loop asks the user a question "What is the result of 2*20 and 4*5" until the user enters 20 as correct answer. The input is taken as a string, so written in "".

3(c)   3 (4 appears three times in given list)

3(d)   k (Last string is 'Shahrukh' and second last character in it is 'k')

4(a)   Since Red is a string, so it should be put in single or double quotes.

4(b)   Semicolon(:) is missing after if condition

4(c)   The index of list elements vary from 0 to length of list-1. So i should vary from 0 to 3 instead of 1 to 4.

4(d)   The string arguments to print function should be in pair of parentheses enclosed in single or double quotes.

5(a) #A program to divide a list into even and odd lists separately

```
l=[1,2,3,4]
e=[]
o=[]
for i in l:
    if i%2==0:
        e.append(i)
    else:
        o.append(i)
print(e)
print(o)
```

5(b) #A program to convert distance in feet to inches, yards and miles

```
d_ft = int(input("Input distance in feet: "))
d_inches = d_ft * 12
d_yards = d_ft / 3.0
d_miles = d_ft / 5280.0

print("The distance in inches is %i inches." % d_inches)
print("The distance in yards is %.2f yards." % d_yards)
print("The distance in miles is %.2f miles." % d_miles)
```

Output:
Input distance in feet: 5
The distance in inches is 60 inches.
The distance in yards is 1.67 yards.
The distance in miles is 0.00 miles.

5(c) A program to find sum of series: $x_1+x_2+....+x_n$.

```
n = int(input("Enter terms: "))
x = int(input("Enter x: "))
t=1
sum = 0
while t<=n:
    sum = sum + x**t
t = t+1
print(sum)
```

Output:

Enter terms: 3

Enter x: 2

12

5(d) #A program to check whether the number is prime or not.

```
n = int(input(' Enter a number'))
if n == 2:
    print(n, " is a prime number")
elif n%2 == 0:
    print(n, " is not a prime number")
else:
    prime=1
i =3
while i<= n/2:
if n % i == 0:
    print(n, 'is not a prime number')
    prime =0
    break
i = i+2
if prime==1:
    print(n, ' is a prime number')
```

Output:

Enter a number: [2]

2 is a prime number

Enter a number: 40

40 is not a prime number

MODEL TEST PAPER 2

Attempt all questions

Maximum Marks 100   Time allowed : 3 Hrs

Q.1(a) Explain various forms of 'if' statement in Python with suitable examples.   (5)

Q.1(b) Explain any 5 operations which can be performed on a list in Python with suitable examples.   (5)

Q.2(a) Explain various relational operators in Python. Explain the functioning of each with suitable examples.   (5)

Q.2(b) Explain difference between break and continue in Python.   (5)

Q.3   Write and explain the output of the following commands in Python: (4×5=20)

    (a) >>> lst = [20,31,42]
          >>> lst[1:2] =[3,4,5,6]
          >>> print(lst)

    (b) >>>8^4<<3%2

    (c) >>> "how was your exam ?". split()

    (d) >>> value=-100
          >>> if value1:
                print("True")
         else:
                print("False")

Q.4   Select the most appropriate answer for the following in Python: (5×2=10)

    (a) Which of the following function returns the hash value of an object?
        i. hash()
        ii. id()
        iii. ord()
        iv. None of these

    (b) Which of the following function returns a floating-point number constructed from a number or a string?
        i. eval()

    ii.   float()

    iii. bin()

    iv. None of these

(c) Consider using open function for opening a file:

        filename = input('Enter a filename : ')

        f1 = open(filename, 'mode')

Which of the following modes is used when a file is to be opened for reading and writing?

    i.   rw

    ii.   w+

    iii. r+

    iv. w

(d) Which of the following is not an option in "selectmode" in Listbox widget?

    i.   browse

    ii.   single

    iii. multiple

    iv. None of these

(e) Which of the following is an event handler?

    i.   action()

    ii.   bind()

    iii. pack()

    iv. None of these

Q.5   (5×10=50)

(a) Write a function in Python which removes duplicate elements from a given list.

(b) Write a program to check whether the given number is an Armstrong number or not. A number is an Armstrong number if the number is equal to the sum of the cube of its digits.

(c) Write a recursive function in Python which finds the number of digits in a positive integer.

(d) Write a program which writes text into a file and prints the total number of characters after reading from the file.

(e) Write a function in Python to count the number of elements in a list within a specified range.

Answers Model Test Paper 2:

1(a) Various forms of 'if' statement in Python:

Simple if condition:

if condition:
if statement block

The statements in if statement block are executed only of the condition is True.

Example: To print the number only if it is less than 100.

```
n=int(input())
if n<100:
    print(n)
```

Output:

For n = 40, 40 will be printed.

For n=101, nothing will be printed.

if-else condition:

if condition:
     if statement block
else:
     else statement block

The statements in if statement block are executed only of the condition is True. Otherwise, the statement block in else part is executed.

Example: To print the square of a number if it is more than 10, cube of the number otherwise.

```
n=int(input())
if n>10:
    print(n**2)
else:
    print(n**3)
```

Output:

For n=11, output will be: **121**

For n=3, output will be: **27**

if-elif ladder

It is also possible that there are many different values of a single variable based on which different set of statements are to be executed which are mutually exclusive, then if-elif ladder is used.

if condition1:

   if statement block 1

elif condition2:

   elif statement block 2

elif condition3:

   elif statement block 3

else:

   else statement block

Example: To print the position (1st, 2nd 3rd) based on a given number, error otherwise.

```
n=int(input())
if n==1:
      print('1st')
elif n==2:
      print('2nd')
elif n==3:
      print('3rd')
else:
      print('error')
```

Output:

For n=1, output ill be: **1st**

For n=9, output will be: **error**

1(b) Various operations on a list in Python are:

(i) list.append : It is used to append the value at the end of the given list.

```
>>>list1 = [1,12,3]
>>>list1.append(5)
>>>list1
[1,12,3,5]
```

(ii) list.sort() to sort the elements in the increasing order.

```
>>>list1.sort()
>>>list1
[1,3,5,12]
```

(iii) We can also reverse the order of the elements of the list using the function list.reverse().

>>>list1.reverse()

>>>list1

[12,5,3,1]

(iv) We can insert a value in the list at a particular index using the function list.insert (index1,value1). Value value1 will be inserted at given index index1 in given list1.

>>>list1.insert(1,7)

>>>list1

[12,7,5,3,1]

(v) We can use the function list.index(value1) to know the index of a particular value. It will return the index of value1.

For example, to find the index of 12 we need to use:

>>>list1.index(12)

0

2(a) In Python, there are many relational operators :

< (less than) : x<y which returns True if value of x is less than value of y.

For example, 4<5 returns True while 3<4 returns False.

<=(less than or equal to) : x<=y which returns True if value of x is less than or equal to the value of y.

For example, 4<=4 returns True while 3<=4 returns False.

>(greater than): x>y which returns True if value of x is greater than value of y.

For example, 14>5 returns True while 3>14 returns False.

>= (greater than or equal to): x>=y which returns True if value of x is greater than or equal to the value of y.

For example, 14>=14 returns True while 13>=4 returns False.

== (equality): x==y which returns True if value of x is equal to value of y.

For example, 40==40 returns True while 13==4 returns False.

!= (inequality): x!=y which return True if value of x is not equal to value of y.

For example, 4!=5 returns True while 4!=4 returns False.

2(b) These both are used in any loop control statement: while or for. break terminates the loop and comes out of the current loop while continue skips the statements in the current loop and moves to execution of the loop with next iteration. For example:

```
for a in range(1,6):
    if a%4==0:
        break
    else:
        print(a,)
```

Output: **1 2 3** since the loop breaks when a is 4.

```
for a in range(1,6):
    if a%4==0:
        continue
    else:
        print(a,)
```

Output: **1 2 3 5** since loop statement print(a,) is skipped when a is 4.

3(a) [20, 3, 4, 5, 6, 42]

3(b) 0

3(c) ['how', 'was', 'your', 'exam', '?']

3(d) True

4(a) (i)

4(b) (ii)

4(c) (iii)

4(d) (iv)

4(e) (ii)

5(a) # A function which removes duplicate elements from a given list.

```
def dup(L):
    u=[ ]
    for i in l:
        if i not in U:
        u.append(i)
```

```
        l=u
        print(l)
    dup([1,2,2,2,3])

    [1,2,3]
```

5(b) # A program to check for Armstrong number

```
n = int(input("Enter n: "))
m = n
sum = 0
while m!=0:
    x = m%10
    sum = sum + x**3
    m = m//10
if sum == n:
    print(n, " is an Armstrong number")
else:
    print(n, " is not an Armstrong number")
```
Output:

For n=153, output will be : **153 is an Armstrong number.**

For n=123, output will be : **123 is not an Armstrong number.**

5 (c) # A recursive function to find number of digits in a positive integer

```
def recur_sum(n):
    if n <= 1:
        return n
    else:
        return n + recur_sum(n-1)
>>> recur_sum(123)
```
6.

5(d) # A program for writing text in a file, finding number of characters.

```
name1 = input('Enter a filename : ')
f1 = open(name1, "w+")
t1="Hello this is to be written in a file:"
f1.write(t1)
f1.close()
```

```
s=0
f1 = open(name1, "r+")
while True:
x1=f1.read()
if x1=="":
    print("Size = ", s)
        break
else:
    print(x1)
    s+=len(x1)
f1.close()
```
Output:

Size = 39

5(e) # A function to find number of elements in a list within a range.

```
def count_range_in_list(li, min, max):
ctr = 0
for x in li:
    if min <= x <= max:
        ctr += 1
return ctr
```

>>>list1 = [10,20,30,40,40,40,70,80,99]
>>>print(count_range_in_list(list1, 40, 100))
6
>>>list2 = ['a','b','c','d','e','f']
>>>print(count_range_in_list(list2, 'a', 'e'))
5

MODEL TEST PAPER 3

Attempt all questions

Maximum Marks 100   Time allowed : 3 Hrs

Q.1 (a) Explain any three functions from math module in Python with suitable examples.   (5)

Q.1 (b) Explain various logical operators in Python with suitable examples.
(5)

Q.2 (a) Explain difference between for and while loop in Python.   (5)

Q.2 (b) Explain difference between formal and actual arguments in a function in Python.   (5)

Q.3   Write and explain the output of the following commands in Python:
(4×5=20)

(a) >>>(20>>3)/8+5%10

(b) >>>x,y=3,4
     >>>print(y<x)

(c) x = 5
     def func(x):
          print('x is', x)
          x = 2
          print('Changed local x to', x)
     func(x)

(d) s = 'listen&understand&query&learn&apply'
     delimiter = '&'
     print(s.split(delimiter))
     print(s)

Q.4   Find out errors in the following programs in Python: (4×5=20)

(a) >>> "How is weather today?

(b)>>>Def func1():
    Print("Error")

(c)>>> (5/(6-5+1))

(d)>>> value1 = '24'
    >>> y = value1+10

Q.5 (4×10=40)

(a) Write a program in Python which finds and prints the largest of three numbers input by user.

(b) Define a class in Python named Cabin which stores number and location of a cabin. Write a program in Python which inputs data about 3 cabins and display the number of the cabins in the given location.

(c) Write a program in Python which prints all the elements in the list who are equal to smallest value.

(d) Write a program in Python which inputs the name of a month and prints the quarter of the year.

Answers to Model Test Paper 3

1(a) math.ceil(23.5) returns the ceiling value **24**

math.floor(23.5) returns the floor value **23**

math.sqrt(25) returns square root of 25 in double 5.0

1(b) There are three logical operators in Python: and, or and not. Logical 'and' is a binary operator which returns False if any one of the operand is False, otherwise, it returns the value of the last True operand or expression. For example, 3 and (4+5) returns 9 since both 3 and (4+5) are True and last one evaluated is (4+5). 45 and (10-10) returns False because 45 is True while (10-10) is zero.

Logical 'or' is a binary operator which returns False if all the operands are False, otherwise it returns the value of the first True operand or expression. For example, 3 or (4+5) returns 3 since this is first operand which is True. It does not evaluate the next operand(s). (10-10) or 45 returns 45 because 45 is one operand which is True after (10-10) which is zero.

Logical '**not**' is a unary operator which returns the negation of the operand. If the operand is True, it returns False and if the operand is False, it returns True. For example, not(45) returns False since 45 is True. not(0) returns True since 0 is False.

2(a) The syntax of for loop is:

for var1 in range (initial_value, terminationg_value, update_value)
if statement block

Corresponding syntax of while loop is:

var1 = initial_value

while var1 <= terminating_value:

while statement block

var1 + = update_value

Here the loop variable variable1 is initialized before while loop. The condition for terminating the loop is given after keyword while. The loop variable is updated within the while loop.

2(b) In Python, a function is defined as:

def function_name(arg1, arg2...):

Function-body

The function name should not be a keyword in Python, it can contain numbers and underscore but should not contain space and it should start with small letter. Any number of arguments can be passed to a function specified as arg1, arg2,...These are called formal arguments since these are only the placeholders for the values for which the function will actually be executed. When the function is called, the values passed are the actual arguments.

For example, a and b are formal arguments in function sum:

```
def sum(a,b):
    print(a+b)
```

When we call this function as sum(30,40), 30 and 40 are actual arguments.

3(a) 5.25

3(b) False, since 4<3 is False.

3(c) x is 5

Changed local x to 2

(Because within the function, value of x has been changed to 2)

3(d) The delimiter for separating the words using split( ) function is '&' here. The output will be:

['listen', 'understand', 'query', 'learn', 'apply']

4(a) Closing double quotes are missing at the end of given string.

4(b) A function is defined using keyword 'def', 'Def' is wrong. The statements in the body of the function should be written with indentation which is missing here in print statement. The print() function is written incorrectly as Print().

4(c) No error. Output will be 2.5.

4(d) Since value1 has a string value. It cannot be added to an integer.

TypeError: Can't convert 'int' object to str implicitly

5(a) # A program in Python which finds and prints the largest of three numbers input by user.

```
num1= int(input('Enter first number: '))
num2= int(input('Enter second number: '))
num3= int(input('Enter third number: '))
if num1 > num2:
    if num1 > num3:
        largest= num1
    else:
        largest= num3
else:
    if num2 > num3:
        largest= num2
```

```
        else:
            largest= num3
        print('Largest = ', largest)
        Output:
```
Enter first number: 34
Enter second number: 43
Enter third number: 134
Largest = 134

5(b)
```
# Class Cabin
class Cabin:
        def __init__(self, number, location):
            self.number = number
            self.location = location
        def display(self):
    print ("Number : ", self.number, ", Location: ", self.location)
    clist=[]
    for var in range(3):
        n=input("Enter number of cabin: ")
        loc=input("Enter location of cabin: ")
        c=Cabin(n,loc)
        clist.append(c)
    input1=input("Enter a location: ")
    s1= []
    for s in clist:
        if s.location==input1:
            s1.append (s.number)
    print(s1)
    Output:
```
Enter number of cabin: A1
Enter location of cabin: A block
Enter number of cabin: A2
Enter location of cabin: A block
Enter number of cabin: B3
Enter location of cabin: B block
Enter a location: A block

Output:

['A1' , 'A2']

5(c) # A program in Python which prints all the elements in the list who are equal to smallest value.

```
list1= [1,2,3,1,1,4]
n=min(list1)
for value in list1:
    if value==n:
        print(value )
```

The output will be all 1s, each on a separate line.

5(d) # a program in Python which inputs the name of a month and prints the quarter of the year.

```
name= input('Enter 3 letters for name of month:')
if name=='Jan' or name== 'Feb' or name== 'Mar' :'
    quarter=1
elif: name== 'Apr' or name== 'May' or name== 'Jun' :
    quarter=2
elif: name== 'Jul' or name== 'Aug' or name== 'Sep' :
    quarter=3
elif: name=='Oct' or name== 'Nov' or name=='Dec' :
    quarter=4
else:
        print('error in input')
print('Quarter : ', quarter)
```

Output:

Enter 3 letters for name of month: Nov

Quarter: 4

MODEL TEST PAPER 4

Attempt all questions

Maximum Marks 100   Time allowed : 3 Hrs

Q.1 (a) Explain nested 'for' statement in Python with a suitable example.

(5)

Q.1 (b) Explain various uses and characteristics of a tuple in Python.

(5)

Q.2 (a) Explain the precedence of all arithmetic operators in Python.

(5)

Q.2 (b) Explain use of any five reserved words in Python with suitable examples. (5)

Q.3 Write and explain the output of the following commands in Python:

(4×5=20)

(a) ```
def f(values):
    values[0] = 4
v = [1, 2, 3]
f(v)
print(v)
```

(b) ```
>>> mywords = ['i am happy', 'i am blessed','i am capable']
>>> for w in mywords[:]:
        if len(w)>9:
            mywords.insert(0,w)
>>> mywords
```

(c) ```
list1 = [1, 2, 3, 0]
list2 = ['Red', 'Green', 'Black']
final_list = list1 + list2
print(final_list)
```

(a) ```
a,b = 30, 50
while b:
    a,b = b,a%b
print (a)
```

Q.4 Select the most appropriate answer for the following in Python:

(5×2=10)

(a) Which of the following statement/method is used to remove an item from a list using index value?

   i. pop( )

   ii. del

   iii. clear( )

   iv. None of these

(b) What is the return type of methods sort() and remove()?

   i. None

   ii. a list

   iii. an item

   iv. Any of these

(c) Which of the following is used to add menu items to a menu?

   i. add_command()

   ii. add_value()

   iii. add_item()

   iv. None of these

(d) Which of the following is used to set the orientation of the scrollbar in a Text widget?

   i. orientation

   ii. Orientation

   iii. orient

   iv. None of these

(e) Which of the following is a widget?

   i. Button

   ii. Label

   iii. Scrollbar

   iv. All of these

Q.5   (5×10=50)

(a) Write a program in Python which prints a given list after reversing it without using reverse() function.

(b) Define a function in Python to get the largest element of the list

(c) Define a function in Python to check whether the given string is a palindrome or not.

(d) Write a program in Python to display the names of the days of the week.

(e) Write a program in Python to write some text and integer values into a file. The filename should be entered by the user. The file should be created if not existing already. If already exists, it should be overwritten.

Answers to Model Test Paper 4

1(a) When one 'for' statement is one of the statement in body of another 'for' statement, it is called nested 'for' statement. For example to create a 2 dimensional array of order 2X3, we need to use nested for statement:

list1=[]

for row in range(2):

    for col in range(3):

        m= int(input())

        list1.append(m)

If the input is **1 2 3 4 5 6**. The 2 dimensional list1 is a list **[[1,2,3], [4,5,6]]**

1(b) All the values separated by comma are packed together in the given sequence in tuple 'data'.

data = 12, 34, 'Googly'

The len() function returns the number of elements in the tuple: 3

When a tuple is packed with some values, it is called tuple packing. In case the values are to be unpacked to different variable given in a sequence, then it is called sequence unpacking. For example,

x,y,z = data

The three variables x,y,z get the values 12,34,'Googly' respectively.

2(a) Please refer to Appendix B

2(b) Please refer to Appendix A

3(a) List v is initialized to [1,2,3]. Function f() changes the 1st value of v to 4.

The output will be: **[4,2,3]**

3(b) The given for loop will execute for all values of list mywords. If the length of the string in the list mywords is found to be more than 9, that string is inserted in the beginning of the list mywords. Thus, first 'i am happy' is inserted in list of mywords in first iteration of the loop because the total length of 'i am happy' is 10(>9). In the next iteration, 'i am blessed' is inserted in the beginning of the recently updated list mywords because the total length of 'i am blessed' is 12(>9). In the next iteration, 'i am capable' is inserted in the beginning of the recently updated list mywords because the total length of 'i am capable' is 12(>9). The output will be:

['i am capable','i am blessed' ,'i am happy' , 'i am happy', 'i am blessed','i am capable']

3(c) **[1, 2, 3, 0,'Red', 'Green', 'Black']**

3(d) **10** (The greatest common divisior of 30 and 50)

4(a) (i)

4(b) (i)

4(c) (iv)

4(d) (iii)

4(e) (iv)

5(a) # A program in Python which prints a given list after reversing it.

```
list1 = [13, 68, 19, 40]
list2= []
for index in range (len(list1)-1, -1, -1):
        list2.append(list1[index])
list1 = list2
print(list1)
```

Here, the index varies from 4-1, i.e. 3 to 0 and the elements are appended in list2 in reverse order from list1. In the end, list1 gets the elements of list2. The output will be: **[40, 19, 68, 13]**

(b) # A function in Python to get the largest element of the list

```
def maxlist(mylist):
        return max(mylist)
print(maxlist([12,56,29,70])
```

The output will be 70

(c) #A function in Python to check whether the given string is a palindrome or not.

```
def isPalindrome(str):
            left_pos = 0
            right_pos = len(str) - 1
            while right_pos >= left_pos:
                if not str[left_pos] == str[right_pos]:
                    return False
                left_pos += 1
                right_pos -= 1
            return True
```

Output:

print(isPalindrome('madam'))

The output will be True

print(isPalindrome('sir'))

The output will be False

(d) Write a program in Python to display the names of the days of the week.

```
x=int(input('Enter a number between 1-7:'))
if x==7:
        print ('sunday')
elif x==6:
        print('monday')
elif x==5:
        print('tuesday')
elif x==4:
        print('wednesday')
elif x==3:
        print('thursday')
elif x==2:
        print('friday')
elif x==1:
        print('saturday')
else:
        print('invalid entry')
```

Output:

Enter a number between 1-7: 6

monday

(e) #A program in Python to write some text and integer values into a file. The filename should be entered by the user. The file should be created if not existing already. If already exists, it should be overwritten.

```
filename = input('Enter a filename : ')
f1 = open(filename, 'w')
t1= input('Enter some text:')
f1.write(t1)
t2=int(input('Enter some integer:'))
f1.write(str(t2))
f1.close()
```

MODEL TEST PAPER 5

Attempt all questions

Maximum Marks 100   Time allowed : 3 Hrs

Q.1 (a) Explain nested 'if' statement in Python with a suitable example.

(5)

Q.1 (b) Explain recursive function in Python with a suitable example.

(5)

Q.2 (a) Explain the precedence of all membership operators in Python.

(5)

Q.2 (b) Explain any five functions for string manipulation in Python

(5)

Q.3 Write and explain the output of the following commands in Python: (30)

      (a) >>>chr(70)

      (b) >>>any(x > 0 for x in [-1,-2,-3,-4])

      (c) >>>globals()

      (d) >>>list(enumerate([1,2,3]))

      (e) >>>mylist=[23,67,90]

          >>>mylist.pop(2)

      (f) >>>len([[1,2],3,4,[5,6]])

Q. 4   (5X10=50)

  (a) Write a Python program to find numbers between 10 and 25(both included) where each digit of a number is an even number.

  (b) Write a program in Python to display the names of the month of the year based on the number of the month.

  (c) Write a program which creates a dictionary of 5 key, value pairs and performs a search for a given key.

  (d) Define a class in Python named City which stores name and state of a city. Write a program in Python which inputs data about 5 cities and display the number of the cities in the given state.

  (e) Write a program in Python which counts and prints the total number of blank spaces in the given text file.

www.ingramcontent.com/pod-product-compliance
Lightning Source LLC
Chambersburg PA
CBHW071207050326
40689CB00011B/2265